SOUL OF THE WEST:
CHRISTIANITY AND
THE GREAT TRADITION

Soul of the West: Christianity and the Great Tradition

David Daintree

Connor Court Publishing

Connor Court Publishing Pty Ltd

Copyright © David Daintree 2015

ALL RIGHTS RESERVED. This book contains material protected under International and Federal Copyright Laws and Treaties. Any unauthorised reprint or use of this material is prohibited. No part of this book may be reproduced or transmitted in any form or by any means, electronic or mechanical, including photocopying, recording, or by any information storage and retrieval system without express written permission from the publisher.

PO Box 224W
Ballarat VIC 3350
sales@connorcourt.com
www.connorcourt.com

ISBN: 9781925138818 (pbk.)

Cover design by Maria Giordano

Cover photo courtesy of iStock (Getty Images) used with permission

Printed in Australia

CONTENTS

1. Introduction	**1**
2. The West after Religion: A Coming of Age?	**7**
Enlightenment	14
The West without God	19
Three stumbling blocks	22
3. The Western Patrimony	**27**
Language	27
Literature	32
Law, philosophy and government	42
Education	47
Music, art and architecture	53
Science	59
Humour	65
Conclusion	67
Acknowledgements	**77**

1

INTRODUCTION

The state is a partnership not only between those who are living, but between those who are living, those who are dead, and those who are to be born. (Edmund Burke)

The chief goal of this monograph is to demonstrate that the West cannot be fully understood without a proper and informed appreciation of its close connection with the Christian religion, and that this connection is profound and indissoluble. The union of the West and Christianity has been as intimate as a marriage, often troubled, frequently strained, but long-lasting and mutually tenacious. Only within the past two or three generations has it been intellectually possible for men and women to question or even ignore its reality. This short work aims to serve as a corrective to the modern failure of vision that observes only superficially, that gazes on the glass and sees only a reflection of itself.

To speak of the West's 'marriage' to Christianity will inevitably raise objections. The nature of the objections will range from polite caution to vehement and uncomprehending denial. At the former polarity there are those who cannot see more than an incidental place for religion in the history of the West. At the other extremity are those sons and daughters of our own age who are utterly without a spark of interest in religion and view it, at best, as a cultural retardant, at worst, as a malign influence for evil. The claim that the West and Christianity have always marched so closely hand-in-hand is meat too strong for many palates.

Before proceeding with an argument as sensitive as this it is a prudent precaution to set down some guiding principles and caveats, for everyone in today's climate who claims a central role for religion will be accused, at some time or other, of racism, sexism, or one of the many chauvinisms with which our world is strewn. These are the stipulations I wish to make:

1. The Judeo-Christian Western tradition has no necessary connection to ethnicity. We are talking about a cultural inheritance that can be and has been adopted by people from every racial and cultural background.[1] The undeniable shifting of the epicentre of that tradition to Europe[2] is a consequence of unconnected historical and geographical circumstances such as the rise of Islam, and the remoteness – and potent resistance – of the pre-existent Hindu, Buddhist and Confucian religious establishments of India and China. Christianity is not a European religion in origin or in essence, but it readily took root in Europe because the human environment happened to be more fertile and receptive, or less hostile, a circumstance that has nothing whatever to do with race and everything to do with culture and accessibility. As a matter of fact Christianity thrived in what we now called the Middle East

---

1 A curious instance of cultural diversity: one of the most distinguished writers of Latin verse in modern times was a Sri Lankan judge, L. W. de Silva who published his collection as *A Garland of the Muses* in Colombo in 1958.

2 In religious matters this may be reversing itself. Christianity is now growing at a much faster rate in third-world countries than it is shrinking in those European and Europe-derived nations that have been traditionally seen as 'core' Christian societies, and many Western communities, including the Australian church, are being 're-evangelised' by clergy from the Third World in response to declining numbers of home-grown ministers.

before the rise of Islam, and the epicentre of Christianity would probably have remained there instead of shifting westwards, if circumstances had been different.

2. Much will be said in this monograph of the 'excellence' of the Western tradition, but I use the term in an absolute rather than relative sense. The West has achieved objectively great things across a wide range of human enterprises, in speaking of which we are not comparing adversely or decrying any other culture. That said, the world *is* in debt to the West for unrivalled and creative innovation in a spectacular range of important cultural areas, and this will be asserted strenuously – wherever it is just, fair and demonstrable. Much current discourse in the West is actively hostile to its own Western tradition, due to a complex set of causes ranging from shame for our past colonial adventures to a fashionable intellectual predisposition to cynicism, an aversion to any notion of objective truth, and a consequent reluctance to make judgements as to value and merit. This monograph rejects such negativity absolutely and insists that the great achievements of the West can and should be acknowledged fully, and that such acknowledgement has no reference to and does not detract from the worthy achievements of other cultures.

3. Very often in this work I have chosen to use the term 'Christianity' as shorthand for 'the Judeo-Christian tradition' *when I speak in historical rather than theological terms*. This may strike Jewish people as an impertinence in need of apology. I explain it like this. There is an extraordinarily close linkage between Christianity and Judaism, a connection that is, perhaps surprisingly, more apparent to Christian thinkers than to Jews. All the founders of the Christian movement were Jews, and the Old Testament was the only Holy Scripture of the Christian

Church until the New Testament canon emerged piecemeal from the collected genuine and spurious writings of the apostolic era, was assessed and collated, and finally gained acceptance by consensus in the first two or three centuries of the Christian era. Moreover throughout the history of Christian liturgy no scripture was ever read as often as the book of the Psalms, which was the early Church's only hymn book, and Christ himself said that he came to fulfill, not change, the Law.[3] So the term Christianity in this context is intended respectfully to include the separate Jewish tradition, while recognising the *historical* dominance in the West of the Christian strand of the Judeo-Christian tradition.

4. A similar comment is needed about the various manifestations of Christianity. To practicing Catholic, Protestant and Orthodox Christians the differences between their theological positions and forms of worship have sometimes looked like unbridgeable chasms, but outsiders see little of that and usually care less. When one speaks of Christianity marching with Western culture one is speaking of the familiar local or regional variant of Christianity in each instance. To focus too closely on one or the other is to enter into intra-faith controversy and lose sight of the whole picture.[4]

---

[3] Matthew 5.17.

[4] It might be argued that Northern Ireland and other sites of internecine Christian strife argue for a different approach, but the essential thing about such a situation is that the conflict is not so much between catholic and protestant as between people on both sides who believe in beating their swords into ploughshares, and those who don't. The same may be said of Islam: any fair discussion of the power and influence of that essentially worthy religion would be demeaned by too close a concern with the differences between Shia and Suni. Similarly let us not blame Buddhism for Pol Pot or for the tyranny of the Myanmar government.

5. It should not be necessary to add, but it probably is, that this monograph is not intended to be a work of evangelisation. Its aim is not to persuade readers of the supposed truths of Christianity, but simply to re-assert the inextricable closeness and mutual supportiveness of the sacred and secular throughout the long history of the West. I am aware that most of my readers entirely appreciate this point, regardless of whether they themselves adhere to any kind of religious persuasion. But I am also aware that there are those whose hostility to religion is such that they are unlikely to be willing to concede any of the points I shall make without the gravest reservations. I can only hope that for the benefit of such readers this work can sharply distinguish between spiritual and broadly cultural issues.

6. That said, it certainly is my purpose to argue that acceptance of the Faith-based tenets of Christianity by men and women of intelligence is entirely consistent with reason and that those of us who are believers are in very good company!

So the aim of this book is not to convert. It is simply to argue for the absolutely primary role played by the Church in the development of the West, not as a mere external resource, but as a central core element. It utterly rejects the notion – so congenial and attractive to the twenty-first century secular mind – that the great achievements of the Christian centuries happened in spite of rather than because of the Church.

2

THE WEST AFTER RELIGION: A COMING OF AGE?

Imagine there's no heaven.
It's easy if you try ...
(John Lennon)

> The clergy successfully preached the doctrines of patience and pusillanimity; the active virtues of society were discouraged; and the last remains of military spirit were buried in the cloister: a large portion of public and private wealth was consecrated to the specious demands of charity and devotion; and the soldiers' pay was lavished on the useless multitudes of both sexes who could only plead the merits of abstinence and chastity. (Edward Gibbon)

It is a consoling thought to many in our world that humanity has outgrown religion. This opinion is particularly widely held in the West, and is therefore of absolutely central importance to a treatise that purports to defend the force of religion in the evolved and still evolving culture of the West. It is fitting and just at this point to set out the principal arguments in support of that view. Together they apparently make a compelling case that deserves respect.

Uniquely among living beings humans have the capacity to think objectively about themselves. They possess a *meta-consciousness*: not only are they conscious, but they are conscious of being conscious and in varying degrees (corresponding no doubt to variations in intelligence) can think objectively about their status in the universe. Accordingly thoughtful human beings have sought to define the world in which they live, its origins, and its relationships to other times and places. These attempts to define our place in the universe amount in effect to theories of history.

Our *meta-consciousness*, our perception of the nature of the world we live in, has undergone radical change during the past five hundred years. If we look at the earliest surviving Western literature we find that Homeric Greeks tended to see their ancestors as mightier than themselves. Not only were they bigger and stronger and braver in warfare, but sometimes they were thought to have been divine in origin, or to have intermarried with gods and goddesses. Later, in Roman times, it was a typical of the ambitious politician to claim some kind of divine ancestry: Julius Caesar, for example, relied on a claim to be descended from the goddess Venus, and following the overthrow of the Republic the practice arose quite quickly of pretending (and no doubt in many cases actually believing) that deceased emperors had been deified and assumed into the pantheon of heaven.

There is very little indication in ancient literature that ordinary people had any conception of progress in the modern sense; times were not getting better, nor was there any expectation that they would, at least not as part of a general trend. The vicissitudes of personal fortune might bring relief or disaster, but in general things were stable. If there were any hope for better times to come in the future it was tenuous and uncertain; the best times in fact were over: the Golden Age had been the age of heroes, and it was definitely past.

Christianity and certain other religions such as Zoroastrianism and some of the other eastern mystic cults such as those associated with the Eleusinian mysteries brought a radical new promise to ordinary people in the ancient world. There was a glimmering of hope for a better future and a life after death. This had not been unknown previously – Egyptian theology promised an after-life and there is ample evidence of such thinking in the pre-historic archaeological record – but such optimism was comparatively rare in antiquity, or at least in those societies that have left us a written account. By the time Christianity had spread to the point of winning acceptance and legal recognition in the early fourth century the thinking of large numbers of ordinary people had been transformed, and not only under the direct influence of Christianity itself but also by some of the previously mentioned cults, as well as by the evolution of a mature paganism. It is only fair to make this point: classical European paganism also matured, from belief in a primitive system of deities, each having a special connection with one of the forces of nature, to a lofty and sophisticated moralistic religion.[5]

It is virtually impossible for ordinary people in Western nations today to imagine the impact of hope on a people raised in hopelessness. Those in modern times who are most likely to have experienced this are the missionaries who brought both the religion and aspects of the culture of the West to peoples

---

5 Cleanthes (331-232 BC), a Stoic, wrote a noble hymn to Zeus which clearly asserts (1) that Zeus is the supreme god (the tone is virtually monotheistic), and (2) that god is not morally neutral, but that he rewards goodness.

who had previously lived in relative deprivation. Missionaries nowadays have a poor reputation in 'progressive' circles, have been the butt of untold jokes, and have been despised as agents of imperialism, so that any claim that they have done good will be most unwelcome to many, but it is easily tested by reading the accounts of those who actually brought medical aid, essential food supplies or education to societies that had previously had restricted or no access to such things. One of the very few missionaries of whom nobody has been able to think of anything damning to say was Albert Schweitzer, whose experience as both a Christian missionary and a medical doctor has been well chronicled and stands as a ready testimony to the good effect of the missions on underprivileged people. Father Damian of Molokai is another. Closer to our own time Mother Teresa of Calcutta, lacking the protection that time and custom sometimes bring, has been bitterly condemned by many who see Christian charity as a subterfuge for imperialism.

It is vitally important in any attempt to evaluate the contribution of the West to the wider world to see missionary endeavour, not only in the nineteenth century but throughout nearly two millennia of our history, in its proper perspective. Let us be clear: *Mission* was an imperative of Christianity from the beginning.[6] The modern leftist sceptic finds it insufferable that missionaries claimed to improve the lives and cultures of those they worked among, yet the work of Schweitzer (and innumerable others) makes clear the unpalatable truth that they did indeed bring great benefits. When we read of the mass conversions of tribes and nations to Christianity we take refuge in the thought that they

---

6 Matthew's Gospel, 28:19: 'Go ye therefore, and teach all nations, baptising them in the name of the Father, and of the Son, and of the Holy Ghost'.

took place under compulsion. Sometimes indeed they were, but there is ample evidence that nations as well as individuals exercised free will under the influence of impassioned and dedicated apostles and evangelists.[7] In an age of individualism such as our own it is hard to appreciate that sense of community that might induce a people to convert en masse in solidarity with their monarch. To us it looks as if they are under compulsion for we struggle to understand the bonds of loyalty that could unite people more 'primitive' than ourselves. But that such mass voluntary conversions took place in late antiquity and the Middle Ages is clear, and the fact that similar things happened in Africa and the South Pacific at the very threshold of modernity may be taken as confirmation that such movements are indeed possible. One has only to visit nations such as Samoa to recognise Christianity as a popular and voluntary commitment of the hearts and minds of the people.

I have striven to make the point that the work of missionaries was not confined to the nineteenth century, and that there is no necessary connection between the missionary movement and the materialistic expansionism of Western nations during that era. Certainly there is a relationship, and the reputation of missionaries has suffered acutely because of that, and sometimes with justice. But the honest observer must endeavor to discern between spiritual, ethical and materialistic motives. Missionary work, with the simple goal of teaching the Gospel, began in apostolic times and continues to the present.

---

7 Charlemagne notoriously compelled the Saxon tribes to receive baptism. It is reported that he executed thousands who declined to comply – and was criticised for doing so by his own minister Alcuin. On the other hand Bede is clear that King Ethelbert and others did not use force; for Bede conversion depended on persuasion and example.

With Christianity in the West came an emergent sense of hope and expectation. Not necessarily hope for betterment in this world, though that aspect began to assume a place in people's thinking, but hope for the fruits of Christ's redemption, for salvation and everlasting life. It is in this context that one must try to understand the apparent indifference of earlier societies (until almost our own age) to the institution of slavery or to the at times almost servile status of women: throughout most of human history there is very little evidence of active and thoughtful opposition to slavery *as an institution*, though there is evidence of individual acts of kindness or of generalised sympathy towards slaves.[8]

It seems amazing to us that an institution so pervasive could not evoke demands for its abolition, especially among its victims, yet signs of such reactions are comparatively rare. Even the well-attested Slave Revolt under Spartacus (73-71 BC) probably lacked a principled philosophical underpinning: if it had succeeded would the freed slaves eventually have become slave owners themselves? I think it likely. Kinder ones perhaps than their own former owners had been, but still indulgent towards an institution that must have seemed inseparable from the human condition.

This same understanding existed among Christians, many of whom were themselves slaves. Aristocratic Roman pagans actually tended to dismiss Christianity as a religion for slaves, followers of a man who had died a slave's death. Not only Christians but ethical pagans moved towards amelioration in the treatment of slaves, kinder living conditions and frequent

---

[8] St Paul's Epistle to Philemon provides an interesting example of attitudes to slavery. He has returned a slave, Onesimus, to his legal owner with a plea not only for good treatment but for recognition as a brother in Christ.

manumission, but if anyone thought of actually banning the institution by legal process there is no record of it until the Cappadocian Father, St Gregory of Nyssa (c. 335-394) expressly called for its abolition. For most Christians, though, there would be an end to slavery, but it would be in the world to come.[9]

In hindsight this passive acquiescence in what we now universally accept as an evil institution seems depressingly incomprehensible. It may help us understand it better if we remind ourselves that in the United States, a society kindred to our own, slavery was legal and widely practiced until the second half on the nineteenth century. Entrenched interests are very good at self-justification, especially when personal fortunes are at stake. If we were to propose an end to usury at a convention of bankers, or if we advocated universal vegetarianism at a butchers' picnic, such notions would be greeted with anger and mockery. If we were to go further and threaten people's livelihoods reactions would be uglier and more dangerous. Slavery as an institution was in fact strongly and unambiguously condemned by decrees of Popes Paul III, Urban VIII and Pius IX, but the writ of popes has never run as far as we might hope when opposed by powerful business interests.

Roman society in general held women in high regard and women could have high status among men, but women's liberation as a broad-based movement was yet unborn and virtually inconceivable.[10] This too disappoints us. In our own generation

---

[9] In practice if not in theory some individuals such as the Jesuit Peter Claver (1581-1654) found slavery utterly repugnant and did everything possible to relieve the conditions of the African slaves in Colombia.

[10] The Romans seem to have higher regard for women than the Greeks, but it was Aristophanes in the *Lysistrata* who probably came closest to describing militant feminism. Sadly, *Lysistrata* is only a comedy.

we have come to accept the equality of women in every field of endeavour. We have seen professions such as Medicine, once the almost exclusive domain of men, not only opened to women but now having a majority of female practitioners, at least in Western countries.[11] Contrary perhaps to our expectations there appear to have been more opportunities for personal advancement and fulfilment open to women in the ancient and medieval worlds than we find in the early modern period, a time that coincides with the closure of women's religious orders in northern Europe, but we have to wait till the nineteenth century was well advanced before the tide flowed powerfully. It must be conceded that the present status of women in the Western world is completely unprecedented in the history of humanity. It is certainly an area in which true and measurable progress has manifestly occurred.

Enlightenment

The Enlightenment was a hugely important development in the consciousness of the West, an emergent world view so complicated as to defy easy or clean-cut definition. It is generally credited with bringing about a radical shift in human thinking; the epicentre of life, it is claimed, shifted from God to man himself. 'Man', in Protagoras's words, was once more 'the measure of all things'.

How did this change in thinking come about and what did it presage?

---

[11] Dorothea Erxleben seems to have been the first female medical practitioner in modern Europe. By special permission of Frederick the Great she received her degree from the University of Halle in 1754. With less certainty it is claimed that a woman named Trotula held the chair of Medicine at Salerno in the twelfth century.

The *Age of Enlightenment* is usually dated from the late sixteenth century to the era of the French Revolution. Among its most prominent luminaries are the Englishmen John Locke and Isaac Newton and the Frenchmen Voltaire (François-Marie Arouet) and Denis Diderot. Locke and Newton were Christian believers of the protestant persuasion, not necessarily orthodox in the strictest Trinitarian sense, but unquestionably devout and prayerful men. They had no quarrel with Christianity as such, though they were hostile to its Catholic manifestation. Voltaire and Diderot were antipathetic not only towards Catholicism but towards Christianity in general; both held a purely materialistic view of the universe. And herein lies the first of those complications alluded to above. The Enlightenment followed close on the heels of the Reformation and was in essence a reaction against the established Catholic view of the world. The Enlightenment was therefore not intrinsically anti-religious, though individual thinkers of the Enlightenment could be found anywhere on the polarity between atheist materialism and slightly heterodox Christianity. In fact the possibility of the elevation of humanity to a higher status (or its restoration to that status after the Fall) had always been part of Christian doctrine, so that Enlightenment thinking on that point could be squared with orthodox theology.[12] The Christian doctrine of theosis or deification, little understood but perfectly orthodox, asserts that man's destiny is to be fully united with God. To this extent at least Enlightenment thinking about the dignity of man might not be entirely inconsistent with Christianity.

---

12 In the ritual of the Mass the priest speaks of mixing water with wine as a symbol of blending humanity with divinity – '... *grant that by the mystery of this water and wine, we may be made partakers of His divine nature Who vouchsafed to be made partaker of our human nature*'.

But Enlightenment thinking probed further into virtually untrodden territory and changed the disposition of human thinking. With the Enlightenment emerged a powerful new idea that Mankind could advance *in this world*, unaided by the divine (if such a force even existed), by the force of its own intellect, and that nations could actually make progress towards a better future. Heaven was no longer a spiritual and celestial goal only; human advancement – perhaps even perfection – was attainable in this life, if not in our generation then as a consequence of the march of progress. The means by which this progress could be made varied, in the minds of its proponents, from Locke's kindly advocacy of reasonable law and the liberty of the individual to the violence of the French Revolution and the notion of class war in Marxism.

It is as difficult for us now to appreciate the extraordinary radicalism of the Enlightenment and its effect on our temperament as it is to understand the reaction of pre-Christian Europe to the coming of the Gospel. A world of apparently changeless institutions, hidebound in its thinking, contentedly devoted to the memory of its ancestors, resistant to change, or worse, seeing no reason to change, is utterly incomprehensible to us who are the inheritors of Enlightenment attitudes. Today a belief in and an addiction to the Enlightenment notion of human progress is the best hope of many in the modern world like John Lennon who have no religious belief, though it is possibly on the wane in a secular world that has been embittered by the experience of devastating wars and the constant fear of nuclear obliteration. It survives in the faith that many ordinary people place in Science, the great Deliverer that has all the answers and will someday heal all diseases and give us all full, long and healthy lives.

As is the case with every other intellectual movement, our attempt to understand both the background to the Enlightenment and its evolution, can readily fall prey to that bane of historians, hindsight. Whether we are believers or unbelievers, our world view has been so heavily impacted by Enlightenment assumptions about the nature of the world that it is almost impossible to break free of the ideas and constraints that formed us and see the train of thought that brought us here. Every time we use expressions like the *Renaissance*, the *Classical World*, the *Middle Ages*, the *Reformation*, and indeed the *Enlightenment* itself, we reveal our commitment to certain categories of thought that are highly favourable to the received orthodoxies of the modern world and obliquely contemptuous of almost everything that preceded it.

The Renaissance as a movement undoubtedly endowed the world with great gifts, but it was also a triumph of spin. Essentially a conservative movement, the Renaissance (literally 're-birth') was driven by a passion to recover the greatness of the classical age, which it understood to be the age in which mankind achieved its noblest work in painting, sculpture, poetry and all the other arts, including the arts of politics and law. It utterly rejected as worthless almost every key component of medieval culture and coined the term *Middle Ages* to cover that whole period between the classical world and its own time. Was ever such a disparaging dismissal so readily endorsed by subsequent ages? The Medieval period in fact produced many great advances not only in the arts but in the sciences too, as modern scholarship now recognises, but the forceful influence of post-Renaissance attitudes almost entirely obliterated or discredited such creativity. Medieval architecture has been perhaps the sole survivor – partial survivor – of hostile spin. Renaissance architects despised it, it is true, and such men as Andrea Palladio saw merit only in the classical styles of antiquity, but even he recognised and depended on the skill of builders nurtured in the medieval tradition. Everything else was cast aside. Not only the philosophy of the schoolmen, but much of the theology, the poetry and the music yielded place to new.[13]

There is a clear link between the Renaissance and the Reformation, though it is a controversial one. Just as the Renaissance believed that it was rejecting inferior 'medieval' models in literature and art and reviving the higher standards of a distant and more perfect age, so Christians particularly in Northern Europe, such as Martin Luther and Jean Calvin, sought to recover what they understood to be the unadorned purity of the Gospels without the accretion of false doctrine and superstition which, it was supposed, had contaminated the simplicity of the original message. Catholics who are also medievalists might well feel doubly aggrieved!

The Enlightenment must be viewed against this backdrop. As we have seen, for some it blazed the trail to atheism, for others it left open a doorway to the divine, though it was generally inimical to the Catholic Church. In the last century there has been some accommodation on both sides, but the truce has been generally uneasy.

We are all heirs to these movements and are profoundly influenced by them, even if we are not fully aware and even if we are temperamentally averse to them. And indeed the Enlightenment

---

[13] A mischievously irreverent but extremely cogent article by James Franklin ('Renaissance Myth', *Quadrant*, 26 November 1982, 51-60) pushes the 'real' renaissance back to the twelfth century and slightingly dismisses the self-promoting claims of such as Petrarch. Modern scholarship has tended only to reinforce the position Franklin then took.

has brought real progress in its train: a prevailing if not yet quite universal antipathy to slavery; the delivery of women in most countries from an ancient state of bondage to full franchise; our rescue by good science from innumerable common diseases that once had the power to kill us but do so no longer; the distribution of riches and the good things of life to even the poorest in society to an extent that earlier generations could scarcely dream of. All these things have brought about a world in which many people can say of God, in the words of Pierre-Simon Laplace, that they have no need of the 'God' hypothesis.

The West without God

Xenophanes (c. 570-475 BC) famously said that if animals could draw, horses would draw 'the shapes of gods to look like horses and oxen ... to look like oxen'. He was highly sceptical about the gods, but appears not to have been an atheist in the modern sense of that word. It is in fact difficult to find unequivocal evidence of truly atheistic opinions in any age prior to the Enlightenment. The Psalmist's claim that 'the fool hath said in his heart there is no god'[14] would not have raised many eyebrows, as far as we can judge, in any period of human history before the birth of modernity. The chief problem in discussing the word atheism is a semantic one. What does it actually mean? Socrates clearly believed in the goodness of a god or gods, but his accusers labeled him an atheist.[15] In the sixteenth century it would be applied

---

14 Psalm 14.1.
15 Plato's *Apology* recounts the death of Socrates in prison, and his defence against the charges brought against him. Its reliability depends on Plato's veracity, but it leaves little reasonable doubt that the master had a pious confidence in some kind of divine goodness and providence.

by Catholics to Protestants with whom they radically disagreed on matters of doctrine and church government, if not on the existence of the deity. In other words it is often used as a term of abuse, rather than a clear assertion that the person so labeled actually denies the existence of God. We first find glimmerings of a mature and thoughtful atheism in the eighteenth century: at last we hear the unequivocal voices of thinkers who assert baldly and fearlessly that there is no unseen world of spirits, that the material world is all we have and all there is. The French Revolution brings into existence the world's first atheistic state.

It would be difficult to overestimate the influence of the intellectual movements culminating in the French Revolution not only on Europe and the West but on the whole world. Since that age atheism, depending upon one's interpretation of the long silence that preceded, has either emerged from repressed obscurity or arisen *ex nihilo* to become a respectable philosophy of life.[16] During the past hundred and fifty years it has taken off and become possibly the dominant opinion in the intellectual and academic life of the West. This is a truly extraordinary thing when viewed against the whole backdrop of human history and it demands respectful consideration by people of all views, for its influence on the West has been profound and it is a central to the present issue.

A survey of the rise of atheism as a belief must necessarily be selective in an undertaking of this size, but certain figures in

---

16 Some readers will object that Buddhism is an atheistic movement of ancient pedigree, but the atheism of Buddhism is somewhat equivocal. Some branches, such as Tibetan Buddhism, are theistic. Buddhism is by no means a materialistic belief, and in that respect it is utterly different to Western philosophical atheism.

the modern and contemporary world serve to illustrate the main lines of the movement.

Darwin is usually named as the archetypal modern thinking man who after a lifetime of reflection chose to reject belief in a benign deity. There is some uncertainty about his final position. The story of his death-bed conversion is almost certainly the myth his family claimed it to be (though if it were true, who could blame him for taking out insurance?), but his later writings appear to reveal some vacillation between belief of a sort and unbelief. Less open to question is the stance of Bertrand Russell, the British philosopher, whose atheism was firm, unambiguous and, one may well say, courageous. In Richard Dawkins we find a more pugnacious atheism, and a barely suppressed anger that is discreditable in the eyes of most of his critics, though he apparently has a gentler side.[17]

The German philosopher Joachim Kahl (born 1941) was ordained a pastor in the Lutheran Church but 'lost his faith' and left the Church in 1967. His book *The Misery of Christianity or a Plea for Humanity without God* appeared in English in 1971.[18] In it he argues uncompromisingly that Christianity as a belief is fatally flawed root and branch, that no good can ever come of it, and that all the good that has emerged in the West has done so in spite of the influence of the Church and its doctrines. At the time he left the Church he became a communist, but has since resiled to the point at which he would describe himself as a classical atheist in the tradition of the Enlightenment. As an ex-Christian

---

17 Calling Pope Benedict 'a leering old villain in a frock' was somewhat ungracious, though if Douglas Murray is right he has a kinder side ('An Anglican Atheist', *Spectator*, 14 September 2013).

18 Original title *Das Elend des Christentums oder Plädoyer für eine Humanität ohne Gott*.

minister, fully formed in the biblical and protestant tradition, Kahl is a powerful and authoritative opponent of theism and organised religion, but interestingly he has no time at all for the 'new atheism' of Richard Dawkins whose 'brash approach', he says, 'reveals a bottomless ignorance of religion … combined with a fatal misunderstanding of the historical developments and conceptual complexities of these areas'.

Kahl is a distinguished exponent of mature atheism. But above all his is a Western mind. His criticism of Dawkins cited above, with his complaint about Dawkins's 'misunderstanding of historical developments', reveals his belief that the richly-patterned tradition of the West cannot be properly understood by those who fail to discern the many threads that make up the weave. It is not necessary to believe in God to recognise and acknowledge the important part played by institutional Christianity throughout the whole history of the West. It is not even necessary to believe, as Kahl certainly does not, that the contribution of the institutional Church to the West has been benign. But it is essential to understand the parts that the Church has played, and to acknowledge that for many, though not all, of the key thinkers of the Western Tradition the Christian Faith was true, compelling and precious.

Three stumbling blocks[19]

Many today who find Christianity unappealing point to episodes in the history of the Church that they find repugnant. Several

---

19 '*And whosoever shall be a stumbling block to one of these little ones that believe in me, it would be better for him if a millstone were hanged about his neck, and he were cast into the sea*'. Mark 9:42.

of these – missionary activity in third-world countries, the persistence of slavery and discrimination against women – have been noted already. Three more stand out as particularly odious to many: the Crusades, the Inquisition, and the maltreatment of Jews. Let us examine these issues one by one.

It is often supposed that when Pope Urban II launched the First Crusade in 1095 he was declaring an unjust war against a defenceless and peace-loving enemy. This is not borne out by a close examination of the historical background. What is very often disregarded is the fact that Islamic armies invaded Italy repeatedly from the late ninth to the early eleventh century and occupied parts of that country, particularly Sicily and the south, for protracted periods. But the north also suffered: Genoa was invaded as late as 1002 and Pisa two years later. The call to the First Crusade must therefore be seen against a backdrop of almost universal fear and suspicion of Islam, the consequence of over two centuries of aggression by Saracen forces on European soil. This aggression did not end with the Crusades, but continued throughout the high Middles Ages and into the modern era. Constantinople fell in 1453 after holding out for centuries, the Battle of Lepanto (1571) saw an end to Muslim ambitions in the Mediterranean, but Islamic forces still intermittently threatened Western cities such as Vienna a century later. The modern world has come to see Europe as the world's bully, but this was not always so. Europe lived in fear of Islamic aggression for centuries from the time of the Crusades until almost the modern era and Turkey's defeat in the First World War. The fact is that the Crusades, like most wars in human history, saw brutality on both sides and many deeds that would now be classified as war crimes caused immense suffering.[20] As always, one invites the charge of racism by dwelling on the aggression of Islam, and there seems little doubt that these issues are skirted in the West by many sensitive souls who fear to cause offence, but it is grossly unjust to both sides to leave the picture incomplete.

The Inquisition was established during the twelfth century to combat heresy. It underwent numerous transformations of character and purpose over eight centuries until 1904, when its name was formally changed to The Holy Office. The reputation of the Inquisition has been dreadful, particularly in Protestant countries, and the Spanish Inquisition has stood out as specially vile in the popular imagination. Caution is called for in making assessments of this kind and modern scholarship has shifted: those who hold strong and unexamined opinions about the Inquisition are often surprised to find that the historian Henry Kamen demonstrated that the prisons of the Spanish Inquisition were more humane than the contemporary state-run institutions, and that defendants in criminal and civil matters often preferred to have their cases heard in the Inquisitorial courts.[21] This is said not to dismiss the excesses of the Inquisition, but to insist that the picture is not so dark as has been commonly supposed. The fact that the Spanish Inquisition, unlike the Roman, directly worked under the protection and authority of the Spanish state also illustrates the complexity of the relationship between church and state

---

20 When the Crusaders took Jerusalem in 1099 there was a wholesale slaughter of civilians, Muslim, Jewish *and Christian*. It is not a contradiction, though it is certainly tragic, that a movement inspired by high motives can be subverted by greed and lust for vengeance.

21 *The Spanish Inquisition: An Historical Revision*, 1965.

that is the theme of this book. We have already spoken of the tares among the wheat. Christians think of the Church as being divine in origin and very human in its functioning. Agnostics will dispute the first half of that claim, but all should agree on the second: human institutions may do much good, but they must be ever vigilant against corruption. And when politics starts to drive religion, the first casualty is holiness.

In May 1096 mobs of armed men on their way to take part in the First Crusade carried out a series of massacres of Jews in German cities. At Spier early in the month the Bishop and his staff resisted the onslaught and managed to protect most of the Jewish population, though a dozen were killed. The Bishop even managed to apprehend and punish some of the murderers. On 18 May the blooded mob, now more determined and better organised, arrived at Worms. Here the Bishop gave shelter to the Jews in his palace, but the gates were forced and on this occasion five hundred were killed. At Mainz on 26 May sympathisers treacherously opened the gates of the city that had been locked on the orders of the Archbishop. The Crusaders then defied the Archbishop and carried out an even greater pogrom.[22] There is no denying that such horrific episodes as these could and did occur throughout Europe, and in almost every period of history. To make excuses for any such incident is to trivialise it, and the modern tendency is to stand ashamed and speechless, and to apologise. But, though it is nowadays adjudged almost heresy to say so, apologies are cheap and can themselves trivialise the very deeds for which they hope to make amends, if such

---

22 For an account of these and other massacres see the chapter 'The German Crusade' in S. Runciman, *A History of the Crusades*, vol. I, Book 3. Germany, of course, was by no means the only site of such horrors.

apologies are grounded on ignorance. When that ignorance is wilful, a consequence of refusing to examine and discern the facts, such apologies are reprehensible. Before we apologise for acts such as these let us give justice where it is due and, without shying away from the sad truth that much anti-Jewish sentiment stemmed from a too literal and superstitious belief that Jews were Christ-slayers,[23] let us acknowledge three things:

1. In many places and at many periods in European history Jewish communities not only survived, but thrived and lived in harmony with their Christian neighbours;
2. Antipathy towards Jews ostensibly inspired by religion was often a cover for ignoble envy and greed. Jewish commercial success then, as even now, could excite the nastiest reactions among poor people eager to blame others for their own relatively low status;
3. The element in society most likely to defend the Jews against persecution were the Bishops and higher clergy. They did not always do so, and some were became active persecutors, but they were the best resource available and some were outstanding in their faithfulness.

---

23 'And all the people said, "His blood shall be on us and on our children!"' Matthew 27:25.

3

THE WESTERN PATRIMONY

The term *patrimony* refers to our shared inheritance, the outstanding civilised and civilising achievements of the West. In the previous section we considered the arguments for a kind of de-christianised West, a post-Christian society deracinated and freed from the encumbrance of its past. In this central section we shall explore the positive influence of Christianity in several different fields that are primary structural components of our complex culture. We shall argue that the part played by Christianity in these areas has been neither ancillary nor supplementary, but literally essential: Western civilisation has been Christian in its very essence. Those who would understand the West cannot sift the Christianity out of it, much as some might want to do so if it were possible. Obviously the choice of fields is not exhaustive: it is inevitably restricted by the scope of a monograph. To many grand achievements and wonderful enterprises this short work can only point the way.

Language

Language is the blood of the soul into which thoughts run and out of which they grow. (Oliver Wendell Holmes)

To many in the Anglosphere language, viewed as a human phenomenon, may seem an unlikely place to start, for most of us share a certain assumption, not to say presumption, that everything worthwhile has either been written in English or is available in an English translation. Language, by which we mean the English language, is as the air we breath: if we think about it at all we do so without examination or profundity. This insouciant smugness, so offensive to many in the non-anglophone world, is so well entrenched among us as generally to escape our own notice. Its consequences are a lack of commitment to studying foreign languages seriously,[24] and a lack of real empathy for alien cultures. This is no light matter. It is for example very common to find 'experts' on Islam have not troubled to learn Arabic, nor (amazingly) seen any good reason to attempt it. Worse, many such people have actually achieved recognition as reliable authorities by the political and media establishments. Yet a moment's thought will convince us that nobody who was unable to read and understand English could possibly appreciate the nuances of intellectual and political life in the English-speaking world. Accepting this, how can we be so blind in our approach to other societies? This is not a petty matter: language is very important indeed and we do well to ask ourselves whether the recent history of the Middle East would have been different if our leaders had been better informed and better advised. That the 'Arab Spring' was likely to become distinctly autumnal must have been obvious to any intelligent Arabic reader familiar with agendas of the principal parties involved.

If the power of language is the defining characteristic

---

[24] Said with apologies to modern language teachers who swim against the current and struggle to find adequate classroom time to do their difficult job as thoroughly as it demands.

of humanity, one language in particular – Latin – was the principal vehicle of Western civilisation throughout almost all the twenty centuries of its existence. Until fairly recent times a reasonable mastery of Latin was considered one of the essential characteristics of the educated person in any nation where Western culture prevailed. Those who wish to play down the importance of this may take comfort from Ben Jonson's remark that Shakespeare had 'small Latin and less Greek', but the fact remains that Shakespeare the grammar school boy actually had quite a lot of Latin, and that his plays are rich in not only in ancient mythology but in orthodox Christian imagery,[25] and that these are, as it were, packaged together as the cultural substrate underpinning his entire world view.

The Latin that reached the non-Latin speaking regions of Western Europe and prevailed in the Italian homeland was shaped and profoundly influenced by Christianity. Confining our attention to Britain and Ireland, we learn that Latin was introduced by the Roman conquerors and settlers during the period of occupation, and by the representatives of the Church thereafter. Even during the Roman occupation a growing Christian community in the Romano-Celtic population impacted the language and culture. In the centuries that followed the 1066 Norman conquest more Latin vocabulary was introduced into the English vernacular, though much of it by this time had been

---

25 Shakespeare was at Stratford Grammar School for about seven years. Grammar means Latin grammar; teaching English was not regarded as a function of school in those days! At school he would certainly have read selections from the commoner classical writers such as Ovid and Virgil, Caesar and Livy.

adapted through the intermediary of French, itself a language in the process of change and almost entirely of Latin origin.[26]

An examination of the word stock of English reveals that at least three-quarters are derived directly or indirectly from Latin. English is a Germanic language and it is thus not surprising that four or five hundred of the commonest words we speak are of Anglo-Saxon or other Germanic origin. Our language thus resembles a Germanic skeleton that has been fleshed out with Latin. When we take a closer look at English vocabulary we can identify a number of classes of words that serve to illustrate, in different ways, the interdependency of the native English and Latin Christian cultures. The first group consists of hundreds of Latin words of a theological or religious character that have been adapted to English by relatively minor changes in spelling. A few examples follow (the original Latin word is supplied in brackets after each):

Bishop (*episcopus*),[27] priest (*presbyterus*), deacon (*diaconus*), parson (*persona*), spirit (*spiritus*), advent (*adventus*), trinity (*trinitas*), penitence (*poenitentia*), confirmation (*confirmatio*).

Of greater interest from our point of view are the 'native' English words (words of non-Latin origin) that have themselves undergone a kind of conversion to Christianity and a corresponding modification of their root meanings. Examples are:

---

26 This process yields some quaint doublets in English. *Senior* is a Latin word, and *sir* is exactly the same word modified by its transition through French vocal chords! The 'native' English word is *elder*. *Placid/pleasing* is another example.

27 This word is actually of Greek origin, adapted to and transmitted through Latin: *episcopus*<*episkopos*. There are many other such examples.

soul, ghost, holy, sin, gospel (god spell), hope, belief, trust, good, evil, truth, wisdom.

A third important group belongs to the language of philosophy and abstract thought. There are hundreds of words that make modern philosophical discourse possible whose origin lies in the closely linked areas of Christian theology and scholasticism. Examples are:

entity, essence, substance, subject, object, real, ideal, false, fallacy, simple, double, category.[28]

Taken together these three classes of lexica constitute the majority of our word stock in the areas of thought and cognition. Subtly in some cases, radically in many, the *texture* of the language has been affected by the Christian character of the culture that produced them. This is true of English, but it is also true of the other Western vernaculars that have emerged within the tradition. I should like to illustrate this by two examples that demonstrate the fluid and insubstantial nature of words. The word *ship* has been virtually unchanged in spelling or pronunciation for over 1500 years, yet to our ancestors it denoted a small wooden object propelled by oar or wind, while to us it means a large steel engine-driven conveyance. The only thing the two have in common is water. More germane to our purpose, a word like *mercy* has no moral connotation in a pagan world, and may even indicate weakness or folly, but it is seen as a virtue by Christianity, Judaism and Islam. The meaning of both these words has changed utterly: the former has changed in a

---

[28] Aristotelian and therefore Greek in origin, but appearing in Latin as early as St Augustine.

way that is glaring and obvious if we give it a moment's thought; the latter has changed subtly and may easily escape our notice without deliberate discernment.

Language has many different *registers*: the colloquial registers of everyday conversation and the media vary in some degree from generation to generation; the specialist registers of various trades and activities each have their own technical vocabulary; the academic registers share much in common but will mutate from discipline to discipline according to whether the writer is, for example, a historian or a scientist. A sharp distinction should be made between the colloquial register and most of the others: everyday communication is usually independent of cultural connotation, but intellectual word usage cannot be disengaged from its cultural bedrock.

I conclude that the significance of intelligent speech and writing, when examined in depth and diachronically rather than superficially, cannot be fully appreciated without an informed sensitivity to the Christian foundations of Western intellectual life.

Literature

... if by great authors the many are drawn up into unity, national character is fixed, a people speaks, the past and the future, the East and the West are brought into communication with each other,—if such men are, in a word, the spokesmen and prophets of the human family,—it will not answer to make light of Literature or to neglect its study ... (John Henry Newman)

The literary traditions of the Church and of the West have marched together for two thousand years, sometimes so closely intertwined as to be indistinguishable the one from the other. Certain books in the Western tradition are essential to a proper understanding of the world. The Bible, of course, is the outstanding example.

Nowadays some readers may need to be reminded that *The Bible* is not, as the word appears to imply, a single book, but rather a collection of books written and compiled over a considerable period of time. Moreover there is no full agreement as to its constituent parts: Jews and Christians of all denominations regard the Old Testament as the divinely-inspired word of God, while of course only Christians accord a similar importance to the New Testament.[29] This collection has been venerated by all branches of Christendom[30] from the earliest times as the chief source of liturgy and the object of prayerful meditation. Its importance in the present context, however, lies not in its supposed divine inspiration but in its extraordinary permeation of other literature within the Western tradition. An examination

---

29 The term *Old Testament* is of course in use among Christians only, for whom there is a meaningful contrast with the New Testament. The constituent books were written first in Hebrew. A further group of books, whose originals are in Greek only, regarded as canonical by the Catholic Church, are called the *Apocrypha* by protestants and considered to be of lesser authority. Moreover some, especially protestant, theologians have occasionally sought to excise certain books of the New Testament if they did not appear to accord with their interpretation of scripture.

30 Protestants will sometimes maintain that catholics had little respect for the Bible, but this is easily disproved by the number and distribution of manuscript copies of the whole Bible throughout the medieval period, and by catholic use of Scripture in liturgy. For example the old Roman Breviary provided that priests and religious would recite the entire Psalter each week. The real issue between Catholics and Protestants was translation, the former insistent on scripture being translated under authority and accompanied by approved orthodox commentary or exposition. Protestantism by contrast emphasised the individual's capacity to interpret scripture without human aid.

of any collection of quotations, in English or any other European language, reveals just the tip of the iceberg: its echoes are everywhere.

The famous remark attributed to A.N. Whitehead that all subsequent philosophy has been but a series of footnotes to Plato is well known. The degree to which this is true or otherwise may be left to philosophers to argue, but what is unassailable is the extent to which the chief philosophers of pagan Greece, firstly Plato and later Aristotle, were adopted as a primary resource by Christian thinkers, early and late, their divergent views on the nature of things so profoundly influencing Christians as to represent almost a contamination. *Contamination* may perhaps strike the reader as too strong a term to use, but no other word so well describes the power of Platonism and Aristotelianism, at various times, to shape and nourish the mind of the Christian West. The contamination works both ways, too: throughout most of the long centuries neither philosopher has been readily accessible in the original Greek and their works have been susceptible to distortion.[31]

St Augustine's is an outstanding example of a mind formed by Platonism and never quite freed of its modes of thinking. Augustine's influence has been enormous and pervasive. Maligned by many for his supposedly baneful influence on innocent sexuality (considered to be a primary Good in modern terms), he is nevertheless a colossal figure in the intellectual life of the West, an eminence to be approached with respect by

---

[31] Plato's dialogues purport to convey the teaching of Socrates, who otherwise left no literary remains; Aristotle's surviving works are no more than lecture notes that were known to the Middle Ages only through Arab sources. No disrespect is meant to either Plato or Aristotle in claiming that they were easy targets for 'conversion' by Muslims, Jews and Christians!

believer and non-believer alike. His *Confessions* constituted the world's first psychological autobiography and remain perhaps the greatest; the *City of God* set a standard for Christian apologetics that none can overlook, even those like Edward Gibbon whose view of history was skewed by his dislike of the earlier writer and what he stood for; his sermons[32] have been a staple of Christian spirituality, protestant and catholic.

Boethius (c. 480-525), though less prolific, is a figure of almost equal importance in the intellectual history of the West. When Alfred the Great (reigned 871-899) turned his attention to education he personally translated four works which he deemed to be of primary value: Gregory the Great's *Pastoral Care*, Boethius's *Consolation of Philosophy,* St Augustine's *Soliloquies*, and the first fifty psalms of the Psalter. Additionally translations of Orosius's *Histories against the Pagans*, Bede's *Ecclesiastical History of the English People* and some other extracts from the Old Testament, though no longer considered to be Alfred's own work, nevertheless clearly reflect his priorities. The inclusion of Boethius's chief work underscores that writer's important place in the mind of the West. Boethius is of particular importance in a discussion of this kind, because battle lines have been formed around him due to the fact that his *Consolation* never once mentions Christ or a recognisable Christian God. For this reason sceptics have argued that he was a pagan, not a Christian, and that the overtly Christian theological works also attributed to him are in fact the products of another hand. By contrast Christians, like Alfred, have always claimed him as one of their own. He therefore unwittingly provides us with an almost perfect example of the indissoluble relationship between

---

32 Over 300 survive.

the intellectual life of the West and the Christian religion, and he who will enter the lists and express a view on Boethius must first be thoroughly versed in both sacred and secular history, and must have a firm footing not only in Athens and Rome, but in Jerusalem also.

No discussion of the literary tradition of the West can ignore Dante Alighieri (1265-1321). Like Boethius, Dante tends to be claimed by both sides in the tussle between sacred and secular. Though his formal adherence to Christianity is too overt to be denied, secular scholars typically prefer to stress his independence of mind and his very deliberate placement of certain senior ecclesiastical figures among those in Purgatory or condemned to Hell, for such things are attractive to those who hope to see in Dante the emergence of a modern secular humanistic spirit with which they can feel a comfortable kinship.[33] That is not the only tussle: those who find the Middle Ages unappealing will claim him as a proto-renaissance figure. Yet he is a near contemporary of St Thomas Aquinas (1225-1274), and though he is best known for his Divine Comedy in the Italian vernacular, he also wrote important works in mature and confident scholastic Latin.

The fact that writers like Boethius and Dante can be fought over, as it were, in the cultural wars between those who see the West as essentially secular and those who stress its links with religion only reinforces (in this writer's view) the present thesis: it is impossible to hold an opinion of value on the culture of the West without being well informed about the nature of Christianity.

A final, surprising example of this line of argument is provided

---

[33] Dante chose to be buried in Franciscan habit, surely an indication of his deepest spiritual inclinations.

by none other than Shakespeare. It is probably true to say that most modern English departments are staffed predominantly by religious agnostics, who would be reluctant to concede such a thing, yet there is a substantial body of sound scholarly opinion that claims that Shakespeare was a recusant Catholic.[34] Regardless of the truth or otherwise of a claim like that, outrageous as it no doubt is to some, it is surely incontrovertible that Shakespeare's own upbringing had been heavily influenced by the Christianity of his day, that his work is crammed with allusions to religious themes, and that a sound knowledge of the religious background is essential to the formation of any worthwhile conclusion on the matter.

Hamlet's soliloquy (Act III.3) in which he considers killing Claudius while the latter is praying, but then decides to postpone his revenge until an occasion when Claudius falls into mortal sin, shows a clear understanding of the Christian doctrines of Grace and Judgement:[35]

> ... *And am I then revenged,*
> *To take him in the purging of his soul,*
> *When he is fit and season'd for his passage?*
> *No!*

---

[34] Fr Peter Milward, in Japan, Ms Lucy Beckett, in England, and Dr Colin Jory, in Australia, have all argued this case strongly. Milward's *Shakespeare the Papist*, Ave Maria Florida 2005, puts the case comprehensively. For more on this see http://christianshakespeare.blogspot.com.au

[35] Another example is *Measure for Measure*, which can be read and appreciated on two distinct levels: to many readers it is merely a romantic comedy of sorts, to others a powerful allegory of the divine redemption of the world. Which is correct? Only familiarity with the whole tradition can make a determination.

Up, sword; and know thou a more horrid hent:
When he is drunk asleep, or in his rage,
Or in the incestuous pleasure of his bed;
At game, a-swearing, or about some act
That has no relish of salvation in't;
Then trip him, that his heels may kick at heaven,
And that his soul may be as damn'd and black
As hell, whereto it goes …

These examples, representing some of the loftiest peaks in the main range of Western literature, beg a question. Has there ever been such a thing as a 'canon' of essential Western literature, a syllabus of must-read books that encapsulate the Western Tradition? If so, should we try to recover it, at least in part, and adapt it to the needs of a revitalised modern West? Through most of the centuries till very recent times there was a high degree of agreement on what was considered the basic constitutive diet of the educated person. For the Greeks there was Homer above all and the Homeric tradition inspired to a degree all subsequent writers of pagan Greek antiquity, especially but not exclusively the tragedians Aeschylus, Sophocles and Euripides. For the Romans there was Homer too, and Virgil as well, and a number of other writers regarded as 'classics' by educated men and women. As the pagan world morphed into the medieval one the classics were still there, and were imitated and added to by the ages that followed. Alfred and many like him gave clear preference to the newer Christian classics, but there were always those who read the best pagan authors and indeed the very survival of their works in manuscript form attests to the value that was placed upon them. Today even sceptics would concede a place for the Bible, if only as a literary work, in the canon of Western culture.[36] There, and perhaps only there, is there some agreement.

But there can be no easy agreement on a canon in a Western culture that appears to be in terminal decline. To say that is not to be cynical, or even pessimistic, but merely observant: the time is long passed when we lived together in a monoculture that agreed on the essential components of sound education. The modern concept of a liberal education and the 'Great Books' idea, largely of American origin, clearly stems from a Christian matrix, in which the Bible and some of the classics of Christian literature hold unquestioned place.[37] But such a view of the canon will hardly sit well with that huge sector of modern intellectual life that is firmly agnostic or atheistic, whose members would see sceptics from Lucretius to Dawkins as more deserving of a place in the literary hall of fame than an Augustine or a Chesterton. And many in the scientific world, that universe of ideas that has grown exponentially and accelerated so fantastically throughout the past two centuries, hold a different set of values again.

So agreement on a canon of essential reading for all in the Western tradition, let alone the other major cultural streams,

---

36 So for example English departments might set the Book of Job, in the King James version, as a text worthy of study. No doubt many have seen it as a work of fiction only, though of great artistic and linguistic merit.

37 Mortimer J. Adler is the best known exponent of this educational approach. See his *The Great Conversation: A Reader's Guide to Great Books of the Western World*, Chicago 1952. Some US 'liberal arts' colleges – rather like small single-faculty universities – base their entire teaching programme on the systematic study of perhaps 100 works which they deem to be fundamental to Western culture. The lists may vary from one institution to another, but there is considerable overlap.

looks like a fantasy, a pipe dream. *Tot homines, quot sententiae*: the notions of what constitutes the corpus of great books will be legion.

Can we find a way out of this tangle, in which every person lives in his own cultural bubble, and agree on at least some works of literature that justly deserve recognition as being essential formative elements of our culture? If this can be done, how can it be done? An examination of the manuscript tradition can certainly help us identify some the books that shaped the Western mind. There are some surprises. Without doubt Virgil can claim his place in this canon. From the ninth century onwards manuscripts of his works were by far the most numerous among the secular authors. We can assuredly claim a place for him in the stellar company of Plato, Aristotle, Augustine, Boethius. Dante regarded him as his master, Milton used his *Aeneid* as a model for Paradise Lost, and Tennyson called him the 'wielder of the stateliest measure ever moulded by the lips of man'. As we approach the dawn of modernity the quantity of available literature mushrooms. The number of books in even the largest medieval library could be counted in the hundreds. Nowadays we are overwhelmed by printed material, and the internet has immeasurably facilitated access. Specialisation is no longer a choice: it has been forced upon us by necessity.

We thus inhabit a world in which individuals are culturally alienated from each other. In consequence most modern attempts at framing a canon are heavily weighted towards modern authors, which is hardly surprising, and either fail to recognise or choose to ignore the diachronic and evolutionary character of human culture. They are in a sense two-dimensional: they expose the culture on top, but tend to ignore the process by which it grew.

They are also secular, steadfastly playing down the religious dimension. 'Post-Modern' modes of thought have not been helpful, either: the reluctance to accept a hierarchy of values in literature has meant that school and university syllabuses have been utterly transformed in our own time, downplaying the claimed importance of the 'classics' and elevating less-known works. The motivation behind such changes in attitude may be noble in that there is a desire to accord value to all human creativity, but the consequence is dire in that it has the effect of destroying the common cultural inheritance of the West. If you destroy a monoculture you may for a time end up with a 'multiculture' but you are in danger of finishing with no culture at all.

Undergraduates who enrolled in English I as late as the mid-60s were likely to be introduced cursorily to Anglo-Saxon (even if Beowulf was a bridge too far!) and taught the rudiments of the international phonetic alphabet. They would all read at least one of the Canterbury Tales, commonly the Prologue, and three or four Shakespeare plays. They would read a selection of novels from Fielding's time to the present, and an equally broad range of poetry. In those days it would have been unthinkable that a person could specialise in any branch of English literature without having such a firm and deep foundation to build on. That mode of thinking now seems to have passed from the earth, and it is possible to find specialists in the same university department who apparently have no common cultural ground whatsoever.

This situation is perhaps worst in the anglosphere than in other societies. In our gormless world there is no Académie Française to keep us on the straight and narrow and still no strong sense that our culture is under threat. But there are signs that with the passage of time many of the works now being considered fit for inclusion in the canon will drop out of sight, and that if we are ever to have something approaching an agreed canon it will be a little more elongated in time, a little less mushroom-like in appearance, than any current model.

Law, philosophy and government

Roman, remember by your power to rule the Peoples;
your skills will be these: to impose order upon peace,
to spare the conquered, and to beat down the proud. (Virgil)

It may seem odd to begin a section on the place of religion in the Law, Philosophy and Government in the West with a tag from the pagan Virgil, but Virgil always held a special place in the affections of Western thinkers and his charge to the Romans to rule their world with justice was interpreted throughout the Christian centuries as applying to themselves as the rightful successors of Rome. Dante, for example, uses Virgil's authority to bolster his own sense of being a true Roman, an heir to the great tradition.[38] Virgil saw good government as the primary vocation of the Romans. Roman law and Judeo-Christian morality slipped easily and comfortably into a close relationship as the twin pillars of the law of Europe.

The Common Law of England is rooted in Christianity,[39] though for many people this relationship is objectionable to

---

[38] He develops this at length in the first book of his Latin treatise *De Monarchia*.

[39] For a clear defence of this view see Zimmermann, *God, Locke and Montesquieu: Some Thoughts concerning the Religious Foundations of Modern Constitutionalism*, The Western Australian Jurist, vol. 1, 2010, pp. 1-13.

contemplate and it is probably fair to say that the traditional Christian moral basis of the Common Law has become increasingly opaque to modern students of law. For many secular thinkers in the Law, as in other professions, Christianity has brought more misery than relief, more gloom than joy, more war than peace, more hatred than love.

And – let us be honest – they can produce evidence to support all those opinions. They can point to the matters we discussed above – the Crusades, the use of torture and connivance at capital punishment by the Inquisition, the persecution of the Albigensians, apparent indifference (in some places) to slavery, the treatment of the Jews throughout European history, the fighting in Northern Ireland, the brutish behaviour of certain clergy towards children. Understandably enemies of the Church list abuses such as these as examples of the failure of the vaunted rule of love.

But against that – if they are honest in turn – they will have to acknowledge that all the evil deeds done by men professing themselves Christian have been counter-balanced (I would say outweighed, but let us be cautious) by all the good things that have been done in the name of Christ. The systematic care of the poor, the relief of prisoners, the establishment of hospitals, schools and universities, the self-sacrificing saintliness of many clergy, active resistance to the bullying of civil authorities, the amelioration and ultimately the prohibition of slavery, and the improvement of the lot of women (yes, that too) – all these things have emerged within a society that has been predominantly Christian. Even today, in the shadow land of the post-Christian era, there are many who insist on calling themselves Christians still who have abandoned the Faith but maintain a firm commitment to what they rightly regard as the 'Christian Ethic'. Amnesty International is a good example of precisely that: though founded by a committed Christian, it is now a secular organisation driven and motivated by that same ethic.[40] Moreover the Church itself has been constantly renewed – St Benedict, Alcuin and his contemporaries, the reform of monasticism centring on Cluny, St Francis and St Clare, the Cistercians, the Protestant reformers and the counter-reformers, the rise of Wesleyan Methodism and the resistance by representatives of all denominations (even if not always by the man in the pew) to the excesses of industrialisation have all been responses to the needs of the day.

Caring for the poor – the sense that we actually have a debt to those less fortunate than ourselves – and sorrow for sins – the idea that we should try to make amends for the evil that we've done, an idea that led to so many foundations and charitable institutions in Europe, all these things we owe to the Judeo-Christian tradition. Even those who have lost or never held the Faith retain the conscience. Even when faith is dead, religious modes of thought survive. Ironically, the Christian (and post-Christian) respect for such virtues as generosity to the poor, modesty and humility may hold within it the seeds of its own demise: Marxism found fertile ground in Europe. I do not mean by this that Marxism was an unmitigated evil that battened on the sensitive underbelly of Christian Europe, for many Marxists and their followers have been men and women of genuine conviction and deep dedication to the needs of the

---

40 Peter Benenson (1921-2005) was born a Jew and later converted to Catholic Christianity. Before his death he was partly reconciled to Amnesty International, though differences had emerged over issues such as abortion.

poor, but there is no doubt that a world that had been softened by Christian teaching, and that by and large had lost faith in the divine and succumbed to a materialistic vision of worldly progress, was a perfect target for the never foreseen horrors of the Leninist world view.

Those of us who live in the twenty-first century, inheritors as we are of two millennia of Christian thinking, can easily forget that concepts such as modesty, humility, mercy, pity, love for one's neighbour and humanity in warfare have not always held such a potent place in the human temperament. You won't find them in Homer, though perhaps you'll see the dawning of a new and more enlightened sense of humanity and of the brotherhood of man in Sophocles, Virgil, Cicero and Seneca. But once Christianity bursts through into our world and sheds a new kind of light upon it, a light that has affected our vision even if we cannot see or will not acknowledge it, we hear St Paul (whose very name raises the hackles of many modern men and women, particularly those who have never read him) proclaim an astonishing idea. Had anybody before his time ever soared as high as to make a claim like this?

In Christ there is neither Jew nor Greek, slave nor free, male nor female.[41]

It is a hard truth for many to accept that in antiquity there was no recognition of the intrinsic value of every individual; the belief that each human being has absolute value has been fundamental to Western legal thought, and its modern enemy is the resurgence of the moral relativism that was characteristic of the pagan world. It is no argument at all to protest that

---

41 Galatians 3:28.

not everybody recognises this intrinsic value: those who out of self-interest have chosen to ignore the claims of others – the Stalins and Hitlers of this world – have always known that they were out of line, have always sought to justify their errant beliefs by specious arguments or by the weasel words of expediency.

The greatest complication in our consideration of all of these things arises from the fact that the tares have been sown among the wheat: from the time that Christianity was freed from the burden of civil disability (or worse) in the final years of the Roman Empire a formal adherence to the Church became increasingly attractive to people of all backgrounds. Whether to gain acceptance socially or to further career prospects, significant numbers of people turned to the once-persecuted faith and took its part against the old paganism. This change of heart took root first in the cities and later among the country people (Latin *pagani*) who thus gave their name to stolidly old-fashioned modes of worship. All this means that throughout the long centuries of *Christendom*, and almost up to our own times, good and bad have existed side-by-side under the formal mantle of Christianity. Every reform, every amelioration of the human condition proposed by Christians in good conscience has been opposed by other people professing themselves Christian too. And what makes this even more complex is the fact that opponents of reform have not necessarily acted out of naked greed or deliberate and willful evil, but have attempted to justify their actions, often very sincerely and persuasively, within the framework of Christian thinking. Kings, Popes, Prince-Bishops and feudal lords, slave traders and colonists, Victorian factory owners and modern industrialists have so often convinced themselves and others that their actions have been good for those on the receiving end of their ministrations.

It cannot be doubted that innumerable people from Western nations went out to the poor in their own lands and beyond with a genuine and generous impulse to improve the lives of those they encountered. But it is also true that many others went out to enrich themselves and advance their own prospects. The tendency in modern thought is to devalue the former and concentrate only on the latter. Such a tendency only serves to strengthen the essential thesis of this work: the West is inextricably bound up with Christianity, and a full understanding of the West is dependent on having a *balanced* view of the whole picture.

Education

Every man naturally desires knowledge; but what good is knowledge without fear of God? Indeed a humble rustic who serves God is better than a proud intellectual who neglects his soul to study the course of the stars. (Thomas à Kempis)

… the best that has been thought and said. (Matthew Arnold)

We have seen that the Graeco-Roman world had a far more unified culture than that with which we are today familiar, and that there was a high degree of agreement that certain authors had the status of excellence. They were the classics, the best. This notion was readily carried over by the first Christians, who accepted the idea of cultural hierarchy, contributed writers of their own (above all the Bible), and transmitted the pagan classics to subsequent generations – though not without soul-searching. There was always, and still is, a tension in the Church between what we might call the *sola scriptura* school, whose adherents believe that Scripture alone is sufficient for salvation and therefore the only thing worthy of study, and those who would 'despoil the Egyptians'[42] and borrow the best words and thoughts of their pagan predecessors insofar as they were not repugnant to Christian tenets. This tension is most perfectly illustrated by an anecdote that St Jerome relates about his own spiritual development. He could not abandon his love for the classics, in which he had been imbued, until he had a dream that Christ appeared to him and asked him his persuasion. 'I am a Christian', he said. 'You lie', was the reply, 'you are a Ciceronian'. For Jerome it was one or the other. For Minucius Felix, who wrote one of the earliest apologies for Christianity, God had spoken, albeit darkly, through the mouths of the best of the pagans. Christ was born into a world that had been made ready for him under the Providence of God.

It was in this mental landscape, then, that St Benedict deemed writing to be a fitting activity for his monks – *laborare est orare* – and in the midst of one of Europe's darkest periods made possible the continuance of the tradition of manuscript production. Almost simultaneously[43] Cassiodorus, founder of a unique Christian commune in southern Italy, actively encouraged the study of secular as well as Christian literature.[44]

---

[42] Exodus 3:22, a phrase used by St Augustine referring to the use by Christians of pagan materials.

[43] It was an extraordinary moment in time: St Benedict and Boethius were born in the same year, 480, and Cassiodorus just a few years later in about 485.

[44] His Institutions of Divine and Secular Learning (*Institutiones divinarum et humanarum lectionum*) is the most important manifesto of his educational agenda. He also wrote an extended work on the Liberal Arts (*de artibus et disciplinis artium liberalium*).

Three centuries later Charles the Great – Charlemagne – as a matter of firm policy committed his government to a programme of copying and correcting manuscripts, and extending education through the cathedral schools of his considerable empire. In the ninth century there was thus a rebirth of learning ('the Carolingian Renaissance') whose reality is quite literally tangible and measurable due to the large number of manuscripts that survive from that period or later: the importance of that explosion, that extraordinary florescence, of manuscript production in the ninth century cannot be over-stated.

This great scheme was entrusted to monks of distinguished monasteries such as Tours and Fleury in what we now call France, St Gall in Switzerland, Bobbio in Italy, places that were at that time (before the rise of the universities) the intellectual centres of the West. Working day after day in their *scriptoria* they produced precious books using home-made inks on the treated skins of sheep, goats and calves. Their hands grew weary and their eyes sore as they made the most of the natural light in the cloister. Their slips of the pen, their errors of omission or insertion, their little affectations of spelling vividly point to their humanity. We owe them an incalculable debt.

Now if we count the surviving manuscripts that were written in the ninth century – they are well catalogued and very numerous – we find that scripture, patristics and related commentary prevail, by far, but that the classical authors, chiefly Virgil in pride of place, start to resume their place in the emerging canon of great literature. Put simply, we owe everything we possess of ancient literature and learning to the monks.[45]

---

45 We should not forget, either, that it was they who made copies (admittedly not many!) of the atheist Lucretius, hedonist Catullus, and the lusty *Carmina Burana*. For good background material see , Paul Oskar and Sigrid

It is a challenge for us to appreciate how in the early centuries after the liberation of the Church by Constantine, Christianity and civilisation became indistinguishable, at least in the eyes of outsiders. *Romanitas* ('Romanness') was the quality of being Roman, and therefore civilised – and of being Christian. It was, to those outsiders, an extraordinarily attractive attainment. What a gift for the missionaries, to be received not only as messengers of the Word, but as purveyors of education, of learning, even of style!

Another aspect of the tradition of education in the West that invites our attention is the notion of the Liberal Arts and the associated idea of humanism[46] (*humanitas*). A coherent view of the kind of education appropriate to draw out the potential of free men (*liberi*) first appears in Cicero, in the West, and is taken up and developed by pagan writers from Quintilian to Martianus Capella, and by Christian thinkers such as Augustine and, as we have seen, Cassiodorus. As the Roman empire faded into the medieval centuries three fields of study emerged as fundamental to what we would now call secondary[47] education: grammar, logic and rhetoric. These constituted the *Trivium*, the lower of the liberal arts (*Artes liberales*). They were followed by the four higher arts, the *Quadrivium* – arithmetic, geometry, music,

---

Krämer. *Latin Manuscript Books Before 1600: A List of the Printed Catalogues and Unpublished Inventories of Extant Collections*, vol. 23, Hannover 2007 or B. Munk Olsen, *L'Etude des auteurs classiques latins aux XIe et. XIIe siècles*, Paris 1987.

46 This word has been much distorted by popular usage. It ought not be contrasted with Christianity and applied solely to free-thinking agnosticism.

47 A pretty rough approximation. Even young boys would begin their studies with the trivium which was regarded as the appropriate starting point for anybody privileged to receive an education.

and astronomy. Together these seven liberal arts made up the curriculum of studies judged most suitable for the development of the whole man, the educated human person.

It is perhaps surprising to find a Christian society placing such value on apparently pagan modes of education, but the conflict of interest is more apparent than real. We ought to distinguish between the skills imparted by the liberal arts, and the tools of instruction. Grammar, logic and rhetoric, for example, can be taught through the medium of Scripture and the writings of the Fathers of the Church just as well as through the pagan classics; the quadrivium can be studied within the framework of Christian cosmology.

The appearance of universities is the greatest development in the intellectual history of the West. Their precursors were the Cathedral schools that had been established to provide biblical and theological education for young men with religious vocations, but their scope had been extended by Charlemagne's more ambitious plan to train the future leaders of his empire and to disseminate reliable copies of key texts. The first universities emerged in places like Paris, Bologna, Salamanca and Padua where there were already emergent urban societies with a diversity of interests and needs. For a long time most of the students of such institutions continued to be destined for careers in the Church, but specialist disciplines such as Medicine and Law (both Canon and Civil) found a place in their curricula, as of course did the 'Queen of Sciences', Theology. If most of the students were in minor orders[48] there were many who were there for precisely the same reasons that we have looked at

---

48 Lesser grades or steps in the clerical career path, normally but not invariably leading to ordination to the priesthood.

earlier, the blurring of the boundaries between the sacred and the secular, between Church and State. If taking orders was the path to education, then it may be supposed that many would pursue that course without having much sense of religious vocation. This supposition is supported by the clear presence in university circles in those times of wandering scholars, *goliards* and *vagabonds* whose figures we can trace, albeit more dimly than we would wish, in the copious surviving secular poetry of the age.[49]

No survey of education throughout the great centuries of Christendom can be complete without mentioning the part played by excellent and formidable women. St Helena (mother of Constantine the Great), Monica (mother of St Augustine), Hilda (abbess of Whitby), Hildegard of Bingen, Charlemagne's own sister Gisela (abbess of Chelles), St Catherine of Siena, Julian of Norwich and Teresa of Avila were all powerful and influential in their day.[50] It is arguable that Joan of Arc was executed not because she was a poor weak woman, but because she was a strong one. Aquinas's objection to the ordination of women on the grounds of their 'servile status'[51] may be more sociological than theological, for he speaks of men and women being equal in matters of the soul, and he would certainly have concurred with St Paul's remarks quoted earlier. Aquinas was of course perfectly right: at his time and throughout most of the years of Christendom until almost the present women have suffered various degrees of social disability, amounting in many cases to servility, but there *were* opportunities for advancement

---

49 For a fine account of which see Helen Waddell's *The Wandering Scholars*.
50 Bettany Hughes has written on this. See her website http://www.bettany-hughes.co.uk/divine-women
51 *Summa Theologica* (III Suppl. Q.39) Art. I. 'statum subiectionis' is the term used.

and the Christian world view was capable of accommodating it.[52]

Amazingly the old liberal arts tradition survived into the modern world. Until the last decades of the twentieth century the study of Greats[53] at Oxford centred on the classical historians, philosophers, orators and poets of Greece and Rome, and the expectation was that they would all be read in the original languages. Viewers of *Yes Minister* will recall the exchanges between Bernard and Sir Humphrey, both beneficiaries of the old style of education, and James Hacker, the product of a comprehensive school and a 'new' university, the London School of Economics. By that time the idea of a classical education had become the butt of humour,[54] yet we may reasonably ask whether its multifarious successors better prepare students for specialist training in politics, the professions or public administration.

Music, art and architecture

The final aim and reason of all music is nothing other than the glorification of God and the refreshment of the spirit. (Johann Sebastian Bach)

In our generation the extraordinary view has arisen that art is meant to be challenging and confronting. This would have been as surprising to Jane Austen, who wrote to entertain, delight and

---

52 Witch-hunting was both spasmodic and late, a consequence of scarcity and social disruption. The reformation closed many doors that had previously been open to clever women and could leave them isolated and exposed in their communities.
53 The second half of the four-year undergraduate course in classics.
54 Sometimes the classically educated ruling class cheerfully indulged their own sense of humour. Charles Napier did not actually transmit the one-word message 'peccavi' (I have sinned) after capturing Sindh during the Indian mutiny, but Punch played with it in a world that could readily enjoy such puns.

amuse, as it would have been amazing to Bach who churned out a weekly cantata for the worship of his parish in Leipzig. The real meaning of the word *art* as it has been understood throughout the ages of the West has been closer to *skill* than to any notion that its purpose was to shock or provoke. This connotation has now been almost entirely lost.

Superficially some support for the modern definition may be found in the paintings of Goya or the troubled music of Beethoven, yet there is a vast gulf between painting to teach a moral truth with a passionate political purpose, or singing of one's sorrow with the highest musical skill and awareness, and setting out to shock others by a self-indulgent desire to be different. The art world is sensitive to criticism, and many will find this view objectionable, but it is surely undeniable that creative artists in all media and in every generation before the present would be astounded by the lack of skill shown by many who now claim the title of artist.[55]

It is not immodest of us to say that European creativity has been second to none. The very stones sang out for joy in the great gothic cathedrals and churches, and Western music and art grew out of the notion that the worship of God should be beautiful. Purcell, Bach and Haydn; the Pisani and Donatello; Perugino and Cézanne sang and sculpted and painted for the glory of God.

Architecture is full of instances of that kind of contamination, referred to earlier in the section on Literature, which so complicates the cultural history of the West. When the Church

---

[55] Recently artist Anthony Johnson's work 'Stutter' was selected to win the 25th annual City of Hobart Art Prize. The winning work is a $20 set of galvanised steel shelves purchased from a hardware store. The artistry apparently lies in bending them.

emerged from the era of persecution and Christians were able for the first time to construct dedicated buildings for the purpose of public worship, the model they chose for their most important buildings was the Roman *basilica*. This type of building had a generally large rectangular footprint, was divided lengthwise internally by rows of columns to create clerestories, and had a semi-circular apse on one of the shorter sides facing the main public entrance at the other end. Its purpose was primarily to serve as a law court, though it could be used for other municipal functions. At first sight it was a curious choice of style for the first public cathedrals, but what other model was available? It was in fact effortlessly adapted to Church purposes. In some cases disused secular basilicas were taken over by the Church, but in most cases the new churches were built on the basilica pattern, with only minor adjustments: orientation would be east-west, and the apse would serve nicely as the presbyterium or sanctuary.[56] Sometimes the basilica style would be modified by the addition of a classical colonnaded façade to the main (western) door. There is no evidence that this modification, reminiscent of a pagan temple though it is, struck the early Christians as an embarrassment; perhaps it was another case of 'despoiling the Egyptians'. To use and adapt the vernacular architecture for the worship of God was a natural and comfortable thing. Only the idols within a pagan temple were to be rejected.

The pavement of Siena Cathedral, praised by Vasari for its size and splendour, consists of 59 etched and inlaid marble panels. Notable artists such as Beccafumi and Pinturicchio

---

[56] A frequent embellishment to the apse was a huge mosaic portrait of Christ in judgement – Christos Pankrator – possibly a clue to the ready adoption of the law court model for Christian worship.

contributed images of predictable scriptural themes such as the Massacre of the Innocents, but also of secular subjects. The ten sybils of the Roman world are depicted there too: the sybils are the frenzied mythical prophetesses who were thought to foretell future events. Early Christian apologists readily accepted that they had a part to play in the divine plan of preparing the world for the coming of Christ. There too are images of Thales, Socrates and Euripides. This whole composite work of art is testimony to the symbiosis of pagan and Christian culture. Naturally in this context Christianity is, as it were, the senior partner, but the pagan thread has been comfortably integrated.

One of Rome's most famous buildings, the Pantheon, is emblematic of this curious intermingling of pagan and Christian, sacred and secular. Constructed originally during the Principate of Augustus as a pagan temple dedicated to all the gods, rebuilt after a fire by Hadrian, it was consecrated as a Christian church in 609 and dedicated to St Mary and all the Martyrs. It remains in use as a church and is the resting place of the last kings of modern Italy. It has thus always been a place of worship. Gibbon was scornful of the accretion of Christianity to the relics of paganism, but the important thing from the point of view of our argument is the accretion itself, not the right or wrong of it.

This strange symbiosis of pagan and Christian in art can be seen as it were in reverse in the emergence of the Gothic style. Even for convinced modernists the great gothic churches of the Middle Ages are awesome, for their astonishing skill in construction and inventiveness, if also forbidding and gloomy. It is understandable that modern people sometimes find gothic architecture depressing and gloomy. Gone so often are the gorgeous colours that set them apart from all other buildings, and something as mundane as the bountiful availability nowadays of electric lighting in other public buildings has robbed them of the uniqueness they once had in a world of darkness.

These gigantic architectural florescences, with their soaring columns and pointed arches, are perhaps inspired by the forests of Northern Europe, though nobody can be entirely sure. It is tempting to see in them, too, a reminiscence of the henges of pagan times, in which case we have another example of that startling adaptiveness of the early Christians in responding to their pagan environment. This Gothic style was eventually converted to more secular purposes, becoming the style of choice for many public buildings and town halls throughout Europe such as, for example, the Palazzo Pubblico in Siena, Italy. This crossover between sacred and secular in architecture continues almost to the present age architects such as Augustus Welby Pugin and William Wardell designing both churches and non-religious buildings[57] in the gothic revival style.

So again we see a coalescence of the sacred and secular, and a further confirmation of our thesis that the two cannot be absolutely sundered by anyone wishing to comprehend the cultural inheritance of the West. We ought not allow our judgement to be clouded by a knee-jerk antipathy towards the Pope or the institutional church in general, and to assume that anybody who opposed them was necessarily a free thinker. To walk away from faith and practice because of differences over the teachings of the church or its exercise of authority is a very modern and characteristically individualistic reaction that would seem strange to earlier ages. It is well known that Michelangelo

---

57 For example Pugin's Palace of Westminster interiors and, closer to home, Wardell's Venetian-style ANZ Bank building in central Melbourne.

had huge disagreements with his papal employer, who must have been a most objectionable man, but his personal faith was steadfast:

> *Send Your beloved Graceful Light, let it seek out a slot*
> *Through which to touch my soul; to make my cold heart hot.*
> *May Your warm and lightsome presence, over me prevail.*[58]

A final word about Christian iconography. The earliest depictions of Christ in the West show a figure almost indistinguishable in appearance from a Roman gentleman. Vested in a toga or at least a tunic, often adorned with vine leaves, he shepherds his sheep in tranquility. Nowhere do we see the instruments of his passion. Subsequently, with the legalisation of Christianity, images of Christ as supreme judge begin to appear in the apses of basilica-churches, a possible reminiscence of the legal associations of that type of building. Only later do we see Christ on the cross, though in triumphant guise: he is Christus Rex, the divine king reigning from the tree of salvation.[59] A more dramatic change in the conventions of iconography occurred in the late thirteenth century after the rise of the Franciscan order: for the first time Christ is depicted in torment. Here at last is art truly meant to shock, but the purpose behind it is utterly at variance with the mentality of modern art: this is not shock for its own sake, for titillation or entertainment, but with the goal of inducing sorrow, pity and life-altering repentance.

---

58 Michelangelo, Sonnet 87, translation by permission of Fr P. Stenhouse.
59 Possibly the earliest surviving image of Christ crucified is a wood carving at the western door of Santa Sabina in Rome dating from the fifth century. It is highly stylised.

Science

We are like dwarves standing on the shoulders of giants, for we see more and farther than they, not by the sharpness of our own eyesight or the loftiness of our bodies, but because we are raised up and lifted on high by their colossal greatness. (Bernard of Chartres)

Holy Scripture and Nature are both emanations from the divine word – God. The former is dictated by the Holy Spirit and the latter by God's commands ... to me the works of nature and of God are miraculous. (Galileo Galilei)

Modern science is a child of Christian culture. It is true that many of the discoveries of modern science struggled to gain acceptance, and it is also true that there is a certain cast of mind, common among religious people, that sees no need for any truths beyond what is contained in their tradition or scriptures, but what is also undeniable is that Western scientific curiosity, inventiveness and experimentalism grew up within the embrace of an education system closely allied to the Church, and that many practitioners of science were themselves clergy. It is a complete overstatement to say that the Church as an institution blocked scientific development, though we can concede without contradicting ourselves that particular churchmen from time to time attempted to do so. The general tenor of intellectual life was favourable towards enquiry. This point cannot be stressed enough. There were, and are, two classes of people in the Church: those who live for the sacred alone, and those who have a broader view of God at work in creation.⁶⁰ Yes, some churchmen have vigorously obstructed science, but as many others have encouraged, supported and excelled in it.

We do well to remember that Galileo may have had a problem with the Pope, but that he was a faithful and believing Christian, and that Charles Darwin went up to Cambridge with the intention, at least, of becoming an Anglican priest.

A great deal of material survives to illustrate the complexity of the Galileo affair. Minutes of meetings of the Inquisition, transcripts of interviews and of the trial, correspondence between Galileo and Kepler, correspondence between Robert Cardinal Bellarmine and Paolo Foscarini and a copious accumulation of other documents have all come down to us. Once examined, this evidence may not impress us with the generosity and intelligence of all the Church authorities (Galileo's *Dialogus* was not finally omitted from the Index until 1835!), but it will perhaps persuade us that there was at least a measure of good will on both sides of the dispute, and that many in the Church were disposed to be indulgent towards a scholar of undoubted genius who was himself tactless and abrasive in dealing with lesser mortals. It is arguable that the affair was a dispute among academics (such disputes are often vehement,

---

60 Terminolgy is fraught. We might call this a distinction between *fundamentalists* and *catholics* (with a small c). It is a polarity certainly not confined to Christianity, for it is very marked in Islam and appears also among Jews Buddhists and Hindus. For an attractive alternative view see *Two classes of men; Platonism and English Romantic Thought* by David Newsome, where the contrast is between what he calls platonic and aristotelian mentalities. W S Gilbert took a more flippant view: *How nature always does contrive, Fa, lal la / That every boy and every gal / That's born into the world alive / Is either a little liberal / Or else a little conservative.*

not to say venomous) that escaped from the academic ring and involved spectators, many of them theologians, who would be temperamentally inclined to see Galileo's heliocentric opinions as an assault on the authority of Scripture and the prevailing Aristotelian view of the cosmos. The popular view of a gentle scientist persecuted, threatened with torture and ultimately silenced by an arrogant and ignorant Church is not born out by the evidence. There is no evidence, either, that a stubborn and unrepentant Galileo muttered his dissent before the Inquisitors (*eppur si muove*, 'but it does move'). This is just a delightful myth. By any account, the affair itself was a dismal one, yet one must not lose sight of the whole picture of a society in which such academic disputes could take place at all, in which suppression has not been rigorously maintained, and in which the correct view ultimately prevailed over prejudice and ignorance. But it is also fair to claim that the opposing view was not only held by ignorant and prejudiced men: the surviving evidence shows that Galileo's abler opponents defended a view of the universe that had appeared unassailable for centuries because observable phenomena seemed to confirm it. In retrospect we would say that the idea that the Earth is stable and that it lies at the centre of the mobile universe is obviously absurd, but generations of astronomers had evolved a cosmology that fitted the observed motions of the stars or could be plausibly explained within the prevailing view. The matter should have been handled better by both sides.[61]

---

61 The modern reader looking back on this affair should be careful to note that the dispute between Galileo and the Church had nothing whatever to do with the sphericity of the Earth. That the Earth was a sphere was never in question at any time since antiquity. Dante's view of the physical world was dependent on its being spherical.

Darwin is the single most important figure in the intellectual revolution that has led to the emergence of the modern scientific mind. To many his is the first clear and unambiguous voice of scientific and atheistic rationalism. Just as he is a hero to the secular, by many religious people, particularly those of fundamentalist stamp, he is excoriated as the supreme enemy. On a less lofty intellectual level, it is popularly supposed that if one believes in Evolution one cannot possibly hold religious views.[62] Yet not all Christian people stood against Darwin with the intensity of Wilberforce. In the Catholic world where allegorical interpretations of scripture had been well known and acceptable since the earliest times, exclusively literal interpretations of scripture were not *de rigueur*.

By a curious irony Darwinism was saved from near oblivion by the work of an uncompromisingly Christian scientist, Gregor Mendel, whose lifespan was almost coextensive with Darwin's. Mendel was a priest, and an abbot no less, always in good odour with the Church, who is usually considered the father of the modern science of genetics. By the end of the nineteenth century Darwin's theory of evolution was falling out of favour because of two weaknesses, the unexplained explosion of life forms in the early Cambrian and its incapacity to explain the transmission of traits. Mendel's work provided a sound basis to explain the latter problem and led to the emergence of the modern synthesis that is known as Darwinian Evolution. There is evidence that

---

62 I have been solemnly informed of this 'truth' over the years by more students than I could count! It is evidence of the ascendancy of a shallow, supposedly 'scientific' view of life that almost completely dominates secondary education.

Mendel was aware of Darwin's theory and was in fact opposed to it.[63] Darwin appears not to have known of Mendel.

I submit that a fair re-examination of the disputes surrounding Galileo and Darwin offers an alternative view to the commonly-accepted picture of scientists oppressed and bullied or worse by a narrow-minded Ecclesiastical establishment. There is an equally plausible view that these disputes were disputes between thinkers and scientists about observable phenomena, in an environment that was *generally* tolerant of enquiry, if not always welcoming it, and that difficulties arose only when and if there was perceived to be a threat to the integrity of the Faith. I propose a modern parallel that might help us appreciate the nuance better. The Science of Climate Change, we are told, is 'established'. To question any part of it, particularly that part that insists that humans are responsible for it and have the capacity to stop or even reverse it, is to invite the accusation of being a 'denier'. This, in the modern inquisitorial court of politically correct opinion is a serious charge that has destroyed careers and livelihoods. There have always been bigots and bullies in the West, as in all societies, whether in the Church or out of it. What impresses us about the West is that there has always been enquiry.[64]

It is relatively common among thinkers hostile to Christianity to acknowledge the scientific achievements of Islam and to purport that advances made in Christian Europe were largely dependent on them. As often, there is a grain of truth in this. Arab scholars

---

63 B. E. Bishop, 'Mendel's Opposition to Evolution and Darwin', *Journal of Heredity* (1996) 87.3, 205-13.
64 For a succinct account of the emergence of experimental science see James Hannam, *God's Philosophers: How the Medieval World Laid the Foundations of Modern Science* (2009).

were well placed to take advantage of the splendid civilisation they encountered in the eastern, Greek-speaking, half of the Roman Empire, and such men as Averroes and Avicenna were agents in the transmission of Aristotle to the relatively benighted West at the opportune time to fuel the rise of the universities. Christians would probably say that the availability at that time of Greek materials in translation, as a result of the mediating efforts of Islam, was a Godsend. Certainly these materials were not repudiated by Western scholars such as Thomas Aquinas, but eagerly welcomed.

We turn now to one of the social sciences. At first glance Sociology looks like the ultimate secular discipline. Conceived as an academic subject in the modern world, many would regard it as confirmation of the notion that religion no longer has a role to play in the theory and practice of modern life: mankind has come of age, sociology is the new theology – and the central thesis of this book is blown out of the water. It is apparently the case that most prominent practitioners of Sociology have been non-religious, but there have been important exceptions. Emil Durkheim himself was profoundly influenced by his Jewish background, and modern sociologists such as Kieran Flanagan and Christian Smith, both practicing Christians, have contributed to a realignment of sociological thought with the traditional culture of the West.[65] Weber's influential work on the protestant work ethic is not held in such high regard as it once was, but it further illustrates the point that religion, and in this case protestant Christianity, is grist to a sociologist's mill, that the practice of Christianity directly affects the behavior of

---

65 See for example Kieran Flanagan, *Sociology in Theology: Reflexivity and Belief* and Christian Smith, 'Why Christianity Works: an Emotions-focused Phenomenological Account', *Sociology of Religion* (2007) 68 (2): 165-178.

people and the structure of society. It is well known that Robert Putnam includes prayer in the inventory of social capital, and Durkheim's own nephew Marcel Mauss also wrote on prayer[66] and extended the range of sociology into theological territory, an area considered by many sociologists to be ripe for further development. In summary the science of sociology is by no means the barren field we might expect it to be: there are sociologists of high standing who stand firmly within the Western tradition.

Humour

... when healers try to give foul-tasting medicines to children they first smear the sides of the cup with the sweet golden liquor of honey. (Lucretius)

He will yet fill your mouth with laughter and your lips with shouts of joy. (Book of Job)

To list humour among the patrimony of the West might appear to be the most far-fetched of all the claims made in this book, yet we cannot pass it by. Nothing was sacred to Aristophanes for whom political correctness was an unimaginable concept. In Rome the comedies of Terence and Plautus sugared the pill and lightened the lives of ordinary people.[67] It is often difficult, across the centuries, to recognise humour when we come across it in the monochrome pages of a book, but to imagine the Middle Ages without rollicking high spirits is like visiting a gothic church that has been denuded of its gilding and gorgeous polychrome statuary. As we come closer to our own time it becomes easier to recognise: not only are Shakespeare's comedies full of mirth but

---

66 Marcel Mauss, *On Prayer*, Oxford, 2003.
67 'I am human,' said Terence, 'and nothing human is outside my scope'.

so too are his histories and there is gentle humour to be found even in the tragedies.[68] No doubt Shakespeare was thinking of the humourless when he said of Cassius:

> ... let me have men about me that are fat. Sleek-headed men and such as sleep a-nights. Yond Cassius has a lean and hungry look.

Political incorrectness might have started with Aristophanes but it did not end there. There are few bolder examples of ethnic stereotyping than William of Malmesbury's description of the rush to join the First Crusade:

> Then the Welshman abandoned his hunting, the Scot his relationship with fleas, the Dane his constant boozing, and the Norseman his raw fish.

Nowadays humour is under threat and a man of William's ilk might find himself brought before a discrimination tribunal. We do not advocate cruelty in humour, but surely the post-modern conscience is too tender and too ready to take umbrage.

Geoffrey Chaucer for all his happy wit, had a serious moral purpose in writing *The Canterbury Tales*, and humour was the splendid device he used not only to sugar the pill but to teach his tales and delight his hearers. Sometimes their humour is so rich and so rollicking as to obscure, from us, his underlying good intentions.[69] The same 'middle ages' that produced Chaucer

---

68 POLONIUS: My honorable Lord, I will most humbly take my leave of you. HAMLET: You cannot, sir, take from me any thing that I will more willingly part withal.

69 Chaucer's Retraction: *Now preye I to hem alle that herkne this litel tretys or rede, that if ther be any thynge in it that liketh hem, that therof they thanken oure lord Jhesu Crist, of whom procedeth al wit and al goodnesse. And if ther*

provide us with an attractive parallel from the illustrative arts. Gargoyles point to the other, lighter side of the Western and Christian mind. Chaucer's era was the heyday of the lavishly decorated manuscript with its historiated initials, floral margins and charming miniatures. Like those eager but irreverent Victorian collectors, we can slice them out of their pages and paste them in our albums or frame them as tiny but exquisite works of art, or we can look at them in their context and realise that quaint or pretty or even comical as they are they are there for a purpose other than to amuse: they make the portions of the book they belong to literally memorable. They were, in short, memory aids, freely employed at a time when a good memory was considered the supreme academic attribute. It is refreshing to find humour and scholarship going hand in hand.

Conclusion

A century after a civilization loses its soul it loses its freedom also. That should concern all of us, believers and non-believers alike. (Rabbi Jonathan Sacks)[70]

When a Man stops believing in God he doesn't then believe in nothing, he believes anything. (G. K. Chesterton)

Things fall apart; the centre cannot hold;
Mere anarchy is loosed upon the world ... (W. B. Yeats)

The sole focus of this little book has been on the great civilisation of the West. The word civilisation is used in the singular

---

be any thyng that displese hem, I preye hem also that they arrette it to the defaute of myn unkonnynge, and nat to my wyl, that wolde ful fayn have seyd bettre if I hadde had konnynge.'
70 *Spectator*, 15 June 2013, p. 13.

because it is an organic whole, richly multifaceted perhaps, but interdependent in all its parts and having common origins. This orientation and purpose has been pursued not because we undervalue other cultures, but because the West deserves reappraisal, something that must be done single-mindedly and well. We leave it to others speak of the splendours of other great societies and we acknowledge without reservation the breadth, richness and diversity of human culture and achievement wherever in the world it is to be found. In Australia we recognise the rightness of respectfully studying aboriginal culture as part of our own intellectual paternity, and we respect the integrity of the other cultures that have contributed to this nation's growth, but none of that is to deny the greatness of the West, the high achievements of the common Western culture that is our inheritance. The once-trendy Erich Fromm taught those of us who lived in the sixties that you cannot actually love others if you cannot love yourself. In other words appropriate self-regard is an essential launch pad for the proper and fair evaluation of other people and cultures.

For all its occasional outbursts of patriotic ebullience, Australia today is transfixed and partially paralyzed by cultural uncertainty. We rightly take a collective pride in our ANZAC tradition and we enjoy the image of ourselves as tough, irreverent loners free of the affectations and restraints of the old world. But the public displays of patriotism and the myths of mateship paper over the reality of a society riven by self-doubt, a small enclave of twenty million people mainly of European origin cast adrift in a huge continent on the fringe of Asia, ashamed of our treatment of our aboriginal predecessors, embarrassed by our British institutions, muddled by political correctness. There are those who fear that

Western civilisation is on a suicide course. There are those who would gladly even welcome its demise. Such is our confusion, our lack of confidence as a multicultural nation, that those who speak well of the West are often viewed with suspicion. It is as if our own insecurity and poor self-esteem make praise of the West look insincere and perverse. It is for this reason that the present work began with a series of precautionary stipulations of which one was that we speak of the excellences of the West in an absolute not a comparative sense. It is needful to reiterate this before bringing the monograph to its close, to remind the reader that to praise A should never necessarily entail disprizing B, and to implore balance and circumspection.

Anybody who has ever taught in an Australian school or university will have experienced the disappointment of finding what little value most of our students place upon ideas. So devalued has the very word *idea* become that the preceding sentence may well seem virtually meaningless to some who read it. The extraordinary modern phenomenon of sport, dating back in its present form no more than a couple of hundred years, modified more recently by astonishing financial inducements paid to successful professional athletes, and grafted on to the equally modern cult of celebrity, has totally redirected the aspirations of most young people in the West and beyond. The very best hope of most is to run or swim faster than their peers, to propel balls more cunningly and powerfully, or, failing that, to associate themselves with individuals or 'go for' various teams and enjoy vicariously the glories of sporting excellence.

Now as in all things balance is called for here. There is nothing intrinsically wrong with aspirations such as these. The problem is that an overemphasis on sporting or other physical attainments may result in a neglect of other aspects of the human psyche. One of these is hunger for knowledge. Never in the history of the world has the proportion of educated and literate people in the community been higher than it is today, yet natural inquisitiveness seems to decline from childhood onwards to be replaced so often by a kind of surly and cynical acceptance of whatever is the prevailing fashionable opinion about any matter in the public forum.

This intellectual underdevelopment is not just disappointing, it is dangerous. Ideas are the most powerful things in the world, with huge potential for either good or ill. That all property should be held in common, or that one race of people is more able and thus more worthy of respect than another, or that the state is more important than the individual, are ideas that have done untold harm. Conversely the notions that God is good and that he expects goodness of us, or that all men are brothers, or that telling lies is evil, have all been generally productive of good outcomes. By accepting uncritically ideas that come our way without examining and assessing them for ourselves we make ourselves hostages to fortune: we might stumble into good works, but it is equally possible that we shall be lead grievously astray. Think of those who were moved to free slaves or to stand up to tyrants like Hitler; but think too of those who did the bidding of Pol Pot. All were led by ideas, but what a vast chasm there was between the quality and moral worth of those ideas. We might be inclined to think that it is better to have no ideas at all, to tread the safe path unthinkingly and never risk attaining the heights or plummeting into the depths. But that is a craven ambition unworthy of the great tradition of the West. 'The unexamined life is not worth living', said Plato. We would be hard pressed to think of a better expression of all that is best in the intellectual life of the West. Chesterton develops the thought:

> Ideas are dangerous, but the man to whom they are least dangerous is the man of ideas. He is acquainted with ideas, and moves among them like a lion-tamer. Ideas are dangerous, but the man to whom they are most dangerous is the man of no ideas. The man of no ideas will find the first idea fly to his head like wine to the head of a teetotaller.

Even the most starry-eyed defender of the Great Tradition can be tempted sometimes to ask whether all of this really matters. Here in the land of the long weekend, life can look very beguiling and instant gratification can be achieved without much effort. Why not go with the flow and take it easy? I am aware that much of the ground that I have tried to cover in this short work was worked over more thoroughly just a few generations ago by Christopher Dawson, whose *The Making of Europe* was written in the period following the First World War and reissued in 1946 in the aftermath of the Nazi era. Dawson saw the West teetering on the brink and responded to the challenge with all his formidable powers. Today, however, the Great Tradition is in even greater peril, the more so because the danger is more subtle and beguiling. It is no longer a case of simple confrontation between black and white, of the powers of good and evil being pitted against one another (the Nazi regime was so unconscionably evil that any force that stood against it is bound to look good). Today the West is under threat from an insinuating notion that nothing we gave our hearts to as a society really matters, that values are merely relative things that can change from circumstance to circumstance, and that beauty is just in the eye of the beholder, having no objective reality. Man is no longer the measure of all things, for in a sense no measurement is possible in a post-modern world of absolute relativism.

One of the most interesting developments in the social sciences has been the emergence of the theory of 'Social Capital'. According to this theory social networks have value over and above their component parts. Social capital is a sort of value-added array of non-physical assets that accrues to a well-ordered society and can augment productivity. Though itself an immaterial resource, social capital can be a powerful addition to the wealth of nations.

Those who accept the notion of social capital tend to agree that it is in decline in the West.[71] Good will, a sense of community, a shared determination to advance the common good, cultural interests held in common, these are all aspects of social capital and all are under threat when a society is fragmented. Surely it is no coincidence that while the notion of social capital has been gaining acceptance during the past two decades the supposed advantages of multiculturalism are being increasingly called into question. There are signs that the tide is turning and that there is an emerging will to recover the common inheritance of the West, but how is this to be accomplished and why is it important?

It can be accomplished only by refocusing education towards the essential life skills of communicating clearly and thinking rationally. The current emphasis on specialised vocational

---

[71] See for example Robert Putnam, *Bowling Alone: The Collapse and Revival of American Community*, 2000.

training, even within the oldest and most distinguished universities, is a shocking waste of human resources *unless it is preceded* by a thorough grounding on the cultural bedrock that we have inherited and should share in common. Only thus will young people experience the thrill of enquiry and discovery.

It is important because ideas and self-knowledge are vital matters. We need to know our place in history. If we have no broad grasp of our past we cannot know where we are now or where we are heading. One would have thought that this was so obvious as to need no defending, yet an examination of university curricula reveals an increasing compartmentalisation of knowledge into units and modules with no apparent connection between them, and this trend shows no sign of abating. What is the point of encouraging students to choose a handful of subjects chosen randomly from the smorgasbord of the arts faculty without first learning how to read and write and think *excellently*? Will the man or woman who proceeds straight from school to a specialised course be well equipped for life, or just for immediate and perhaps temporary employment? The Great Tradition of the West is our most precious worldly possession. It has the power to nourish us, but it is a *table d'hôte* not a buffet: you cannot fully appreciate it if you pick and choose the bits you like and leave the rest.

At the outset we promised that this work had no proselytising purpose, though we also claimed that it was reasonable for intelligent persons to hold to the tenets of the Christian religion, and that such people find themselves in very good company. It is fitting to close with an amplification of that claim, while recognising that no proof of God's existence and activity in the world will ever convince those who do not allow the validity of any argument that is based on non-physical, non-measurable phenomena.

However a powerful and complex argument from probability can be constructed from three principal sources: firstly, the reasoning of philosophers and other thinkers, secondly, the evidence of Scripture and the post-apostolic witnesses to the extraordinary emergence *ex nihilo* of the Church into history, and thirdly the anecdotal experience of individual believers. Of the first it need only be said that an objective and comprehensive survey of the views of philosophers in different cultures and different epochs will emphatically exclude the notion that atheism has been their dominant creed. That is simply untrue. On the second point, St Augustine's famous statement *"I would not have believed the gospel, unless the authority of the Catholic Church had induced me"*,[72] though contentious in terms of the dialogue between Catholic and Reformed Christianity, makes it clear that a Christian of the early fifth century could see the witness of Scripture as being at the very least reinforced by the actuality of the assembly of the faithful. On the third point there is potency in the narratives of those who have passed from unbelief to Faith. C. S. Lewis,[73] Anthony Flew,[74] Holly Ordway[75] and Peter Hitchens[76] are useful allies to isolated believers whose friends treat their simple confidence with disdain. Other helpful

---

[72] *Contra Ep. Fund.* V, 6.
[73] *Surprised by Joy.*
[74] *There is a God: How The World's Most Notorious Atheist Changed His Mind*, Antony Flew with Roy Varghese, New York, 2007.
[75] *Not God's Type.*
[76] Brother of the late Christopher Hitchens. The account of his conversion is *Rage Against God: How Atheism led me to Faith.*

aides are the Anglican priest-scientist John Polkinghorne,[77] and Peter Kreeft, whose *Handbook of Christian Apologetics* (1994) lists and provides commentary on no less than 20 of the classical philosophical arguments for the existence of God.[78] A powerful battery indeed.

My principal goals in writing have always been:

1. to demonstrate to readers, regardless of their opinion about the existence or non-existence of a creator God, that belief is intellectually respectable;
2. to show that a full understanding of the Western tradition is not achievable without an appreciation of the contribution of Christianity;
3. to argue that the Western, Christian, tradition has gifted to the whole world an extraordinary and brilliant range of achievements in the arts and sciences, in government and in practical ethics;
4. to insist (without denying the human tendency to fall far short of perfection) that it is not only utterly reasonable to value and respect the great works of the West, but that justice demands such generous recognition.

I do not want to end on a polemical note and am happy to leave the last word to one who was probably not an orthodox

---

[77] See for example *Reason and Reality: The Relationship between Science and Theology, SPCK*, 2011.
[78] Easily available on the internet at http://www.peterkreeft.com/topics-more/20_arguments-gods-existence.htm. His *Letters to an Atheist* is also recommended.

Christian, but whose estimation of the value of the West was comprehensive:

> The whole scope of the essay is to recommend culture as the great help out of our present difficulties; culture being a pursuit of our total perfection by means of getting to know, on all the matters which most concern us, the best which has been thought and said in the world, and, through this knowledge, turning a stream of fresh and free thought upon our stock notions and habits, which we now follow staunchly but mechanically ...[79]

---

[79] Matthew Arnold, *Culture and Anarchy*, from the 1875 Preface.

Acknowledgements

I wish to thank those who have involved me in this project or assisted me with their scholarly advice: Mr John Roskam, Executive Director of the IPA, originally suggested the project to me. One's learning, such as it is, is acquired gradually over a lifetime: I hold close to my heart the memory of all my teachers.